Sh-Boom!
LIFE COULD BE A
DREAM

by **Roger Bean**

STEELE SPRING
STAGE RIGHTS
www.stagerights.com

SH-BOOM! LIFE COULD BE A DREAM

For all stage performance inquiries, please contact:

Steele Spring Stage Rights
3845 Cazador Street
Los Angeles, CA 90065 (323) 739-0413
www.stagerights.com

Sh-Boom!
LIFE COULD BE A
DREAM

written and created by Roger Bean
premiered on September 7, 2007 at Milwaukee Repertory Theater,
Joseph Hanreddy, Artistic Director, Timothy J. Shields, Managing Director,
Sandy Ernst, Associate Artistic Director

Vocal Arrangements by Roger Bean • Orchestrations by Jon Newton
Choreography by Pam Kriger • Musical Direction by Paul Helm
Scenic Design by Susannah Barnes • Costume Design by Rachel Laritz
Lighting Design by Jason Fassl • Stage Manager: Richelle Harrington
Production Manager: Judy Berdan • Direction and Staging by Roger Bean

Cast
Ben Cherry as Denny • Richard Israel as Eugene • Justin Robertson as Wally
Carlos Martin as Duke (Skip) • Julia Graham as Mrs. Varney & Lois

Sh-Boom!
LIFE COULD BE A
DREAM

The Los Angeles production opened on August 7, 2009,
running for one year at the Hudson Mainstage Theatre,
produced by David Elzer, Peter Schneider and Roger Bean

Created and Directed by Roger Bean
Musical Arrangements by Roger Bean & Jon Newton
Additional Musical Arrangements by Steve Parsons
Choreography by Lee Martino • Musical Direction by Michael Paternastro
Scenic Design by Tom Buderwitz • Costume Design by Shon LeBlanc & David Elzer
Lighting Design by Luke Moyer • Sound Design by Cricket S. Myers
Casting by Michael Donovan CSA • Stage Manager: Nate Genung

Cast
Daniel Tatar as Denny • Jim Holdridge as Eugene • Ryan Castellino as Wally
Doug Carpenter as Duke (Skip) • Jessica Keenan Wynn as Mrs. Varney & Lois
with David Engel as the voice of "Bullseye" Miller

Sh-Boom!
LIFE COULD BE A
DREAM

This final version of Sh-Boom! Life Could Be A Dream premiered at Stages Repertory
Theater, Houston, TX. Kenn McLaughlin, Artistic Director; Mark Folkes, Managing
Director. The production was directed and choreographed by Mitchell Greco.

Music Direction by Steven Jones • Musical Arrangements by Michael Borth
Featuring Adam Gibbs, Mark Ivy, Kiaya Scott, Kiefer Slaton, & Cameron Khalil Stokes

SH-BOOM! LIFE COULD BE A DREAM

DENNY VARNEY

Five years after high school graduation, Denny still lives with his mother, goofing off in the family basement instead of working for a living. Denny's lack of ambition and discipline have always been his downfall, but the new WOPR Radio "Dream of a Lifetime Talent Search" has put new wind in his sails. He uses his talents as a former Crooning Crab Cake (the Glee Club at Springfield High) to first create a duo, then a trio, and finally a quartet to help find the unique doo-wop sound (and backer's money) he needs to bring his dream to reality. Jealousy rears its head when the final member of the group unintentionally steals Denny's spotlight. Can Denny still lead the group to a win? Will he still be able to attract the ladies in the spotlight? Stay tuned...

EUGENE JOHNSON

Denny's best friend and co-conspirator, Eugene works hard just to stay in step with Denny's fast-moving schemes. During most days, Eugene works for his Dad down at the Springfield Sweet Shoppe, but at night he cuts loose with his fellow Crooning Crab Cakes during singing and dancing practice in Denny's basement. The entrance of an old grade-school crush, Lois, threatens to derail all attempts at winning the radio contest, and Eugene has to work twice as hard as the others to keep his mind in the game. Does he have a shot at winning the girl back? Can he possibly become a functioning member of the doo-wop Dream group? Stay tuned...

WALLY PATTON

A checker at the Piggly-Wiggly, and older brother to bad-boy Billy Ray (referenced in *The Marvelous Wonderettes*), Wally is the son of a preacher who truly becomes the heart and soul of the group. He's desperate to be a part of Denny's scheme, simply because inclusion seems much better than exclusion. Still a youngster himself, often childish, he does have an uncanny knack for seeing what's important in life when the going gets tough. But that doesn't mean he's not immune to a full-on crush when Eugene's grade-school sweetheart comes into the picture. Does Wally have a shot at the girl? Will the fight over Lois create a rift too wide to repair? Stay tuned...

SH-BOOM! LIFE COULD BE A DREAM (CONT'D)

DUKE HENDERSON
The last add-on to our singing group, Duke is the new guy from the wrong side of the tracks, and a natural singing whiz. He works for Earl's Big Stuff Auto, the new sponsor of the group, and Duke is added to Denny's fledgling group to turn it into a proper quartet. Duke is ruggedly handsome and definitely the new alpha male, and Denny feels pushed aside and ignored for the seemingly brighter talents Duke brings to the table. Duke is conflicted about falling in love with the boss's daughter, Lois, the girl that Eugene and Wally are already fighting over. Could he ever possibly fit into her family? Will Duke's bad-boy attitude break up the group's chance to win the big contest? Stay tuned...

LOIS FRANKLIN
Daughter of Earl Franklin, owner of Earl's Big Stuff Auto, and herself a former song leader at Springfield High, Lois arrives on the scene to help shape the boys into a real singing group. Going against her father's advice, she decides to give his sponsorship money to the fledgling quartet, and in doing so falls head-over-heels in love with bad-boy Duke. Lois' parents refuse to allow their daughter to date the grease monkey from their auto shop, and the fireworks that ensue threaten to destroy the whole enterprise. Will Lois get the guy? Which guy? Can she be the super-glue that holds the whole group together? Stay tuned...

MRS. VARNEY (V.O. LIVE FROM OFFSTAGE – by LOIS)
Denny's offstage mother. ASM portrays her legs onstage. Actress portraying LOIS actually says the lines, live from backstage.

"BULLSEYE" MILLER (V.O.)
Radio DJ / Announcer

TIME & PLACE
Denny's Basement & Onstage at the Springfield Town Hall, 1960-ish

MUSICAL NUMBERS

ACT I

Scene 1 / Monday, just about lunch-time

#1   SH-BOOM (LIFE COULD BE A DREAM) ....Denny, Eugene & Wally

#2   GET A JOB ....Wally, Denny, Eugene & Mrs. Varney

#3   MAMA DON'T ALLOW IT ....Denny, Eugene & Wally

Scene 2 / Tuesday Evening

#4   TEARS ON MY PILLOW ....Eugene, Denny & Wally

#5   FOOLS FALL IN LOVE...All

Scene 3 / Thursday Evening

#6   RUNAROUND SUE...Duke, Denny, Eugene & Wally

#7   LONELY TEARDROPS....................................Duke, Denny, Eugene & Wally

#8   LOVIN' LOIS MEDLEY

       DEVIL OR ANGEL..Wally & Men

       EARTH ANGEL ....Denny & Men

       ONLY YOU..Eugene & Men

       I ONLY HAVE EYES FOR YOU ....Lois & Men

#9   STAY ....Denny, Eugene, Wally & Lois

Scene 4 / Friday Evening

#10   (JUST LIKE) ROMEO AND JULIET ....Denny, Eugene & Wally

#11   A SUNDAY KIND OF LOVE .... Duke w/ Wally

#12   UNCHAINED MELODY.. Lois & Duke w/ Men

MUSICAL NUMBERS

ACT II

#13   ENTR'ACTE ....Band

Scene 1 / Saturday Morning

#14   DREAMIN' ....Denny, Eugene & Wally

#15   EASIER SAID THAN DONE .... Lois w/ Denny, Eugene & Wally

#16   (YOU'VE GOT) THE MAGIC TOUCH .... Denny w/ Eugene & Wally

#17   LONELY TEARDROPS (REPRISE) .... Lois & Duke

Scene 2 / Saturday Afternoon

#18   BUZZ BUZZ BUZZ..Denny, Eugene & Wally

#19   FOOLS FALL IN LOVE (REPRISE)/

    THE GLORY OF LOVE .... Duke, Wally w/ Denny & Eugene

#20   LIFE COULD BE A DREAM (REPRISE)/DUKE OF EARL .... Lois, Duke, All

Scene 3 / Finale

#21   PRETTY LITTLE ANGEL EYES...Denny, All

#22   DO YOU LOVE ME? / THE TWIST .... Eugene, Wally, All

#23   RAMA LAMA DING DONG ....Duke, All

#24   ENCORE: UNCHAINED MELODY (REPRISE) ....Lois, Duke, All

#25   BOWS (SH-BOOM) ....Band

#26   EXIT ....Band

ACT I

SCENE 1

BASEMENT REC ROOM: MONDAY AFTERNOON.

We are in the basement of the Varney home, where Denny lives with his mother. Scattered around the room are various pieces of long-forgotten sports equipment, shelves of trophies and memorabilia, and other items now relegated to basement storage.

One wall is dedicated to pendants and school paraphernalia: "Springfield High School," "Go Chipmunks," and some "Crooning Crab Cakes" memorabilia.

Another wall is dedicated to music, with covers of sheet music, record albums, and at least one guitar on display.

One end of the room houses a wet bar, with a counter and stools. There is a bell hung by the bar, the type that can be rung with a tug of a cord (like a ship's bell). Along one wall there is a radiator, next to a table with a basket of laundry, with a few of Mrs. Varney's clothing items.

Along the top of the set proscenium is a large radio dial that lights up and pulses when the radio announcer speaks.

When creating the set, make sure to have enough room by the entrance door for Mrs. Varney to stand, leaving ample room for her to maneuver out of the way for quick entrances and exits. The door at the top of steps is partially masked, and we can only see Mrs. Varney from the knees down when she enters and stands at the top of the landing.

> **SOUND: In the dark, we hear the radio playing.**

#1: "SH-BOOM: PART 1" (PRE-RECORD)

RADIO (V.O.):
LIFE COULD BE A DREAM
LIFE COULD BE A DREAM

> *LIGHTS up on the radio dial.*

DOO, DOO, DOO, DOO SH-BOOM!

> *LIGHTS slowly rise on the basement.*

DENNY enters, carrying a portable radio. He holds it up to his ear as he crosses down the stairs.

RADIO (V.O.) (CONT'D):
LIFE COULD BE A DREAM
IF I COULD TAKE YOU UP TO PARADISE UP ABOVE

The music continues.

The DJ is heard over the music. He speaks quickly and distinctly, hitting various words for emphasis. He's a big personality, and we hear from him throughout the show.

DISC JOCKEY (V.O.): Hey cool cats— this is 'Bullseye' Miller.

> *SOUND: "Arrow hitting a Bullseye" sound effect.*

Life could be a dream for one lucky singing group out there! Radio Station W-O-P-R— that's Big Whopper Radio...

> *SOUND: Radio Jingle: "Big Whopper Radio." (See Song #2A)*

...is looking for someone with a new, hip sound! If you've got what it takes, sign up this week for the "Dream of a Lifetime" Talent Search. Tune in as we broadcast live this Saturday night at the Big Whopper Radio Rock 'n' Roll Round-up...

> *SOUND: Radio Jingle: "Big Whopper Radio."*

...where our lucky winners will receive a one-year recording contract with yours truly and Bullseye Records!

> *SOUND: "Arrow hitting a Bullseye" sound effect.*

This contest is bound to be the greatest thing since Howdy met Doody! So, take this tip if you want to be hip! Life could be a dream for YOU!!

LIGHTS down on proscenium radio. Music segues to live transition.

#1A: "SH-BOOM: PART 2"

DENNY is beside himself, and puts his portable radio down.

DENNY: Where the heck is that loser-doozer? I have to do everything myself.

DENNY plants himself center for his imaginary audience.

(Singing)
LIFE COULD BE A DREAM
IF I COULD TAKE YOU UP TO PARADISE UP ABOVE

DENNY (CONT'D):
> IF YOU WOULD TELL ME I'M THE ONLY ONE THAT YOU LOVE
> LIFE COULD BE A DREAM SWEETHEART

> > *The door bangs open, and EUGENE rushes in and down the stairs.*

EUGENE: Sorry I'm late, Denny...!

DENNY:
> LIFE COULD BE A DREAM
> I GUESS I'LL HAVE TO WIN THE CONTEST BY MYSELF

EUGENE: It's not my fault! Miss Wilkerson knocked over the Atomic Fireballs again and Dad made me count 'em all before lunchtime. They were all over the place!

DENNY: I don't know, Eugene. You don't seem very dedicated to the contest.

> > *DENNY and EUGENE now face off, and THEY sing back and forth, speaking and arguing with each other while practicing moves.*

DENNY:	**EUGENE:**
SH-BOOM, SH-BOOM	SH-BOOM, SH-BOOM
	(Spoken)
YA-DA-DA-DA-DA-DA-DA-DA-DA-DA	Not fair! I spend every lunch-time here.
	(Singing)
SH-BOOM, SH-BOOM	SH-BOOM, SH-BOOM
(Speaking)	
We won't win unless you're on time!	YA-DA-DA-DA-DA-DA-DA-DA-DA-DA
(Singing)	
SH-BOOM, SH-BOOM	SH-BOOM, SH-BOOM
(Speaking)	*(Speaking)*
Eugene, you're such a loser-doozer!	You need two, so you're stuck with me!

> *Now practically yelling at each other.*

(Singing)	*(Singing)*
SH-BOOM!	SH-BOOM!

> > *MRS. VARNEY opens the door and FLASHES THE LIGHTS.*

LIGHTS: Lights flashing. [Each time Mrs. Varney flashes the lights ALL of the stage lights should go down and up twice— long enough to notice. Then follow with lights up on Mr. Varney's legs, if possible.]

We see her from the knees down. Throughout the play, whenever SHE enters into the scene, we only see her legs.

[The actress portraying LOIS supplies MRS. VARNEY'S voice live from backstage, while an ASM/backstage crewperson portrays MRS. VARNEY's legs.]

MRS. VARNEY (LIVE FROM OFFSTAGE) *(as the lights flash)*: Hello Denny. This is your mother.

DENNY: I know it's you, Ma. You're the only one who flashes the lights. Whattaya want?

MRS. VARNEY (LIVE FROM OFFSTAGE): Did you finish folding the laundry like I asked?

DENNY points to the basket of unfolded laundry.

DENNY: Yes.

MRS. VARNEY (LIVE FROM OFFSTAGE): Well you must be hungry for some lunch now, what with all of the job hunting you did this morning.

EUGENE: Ha!

DENNY smacks EUGENE in the arm.

Ow!

DENNY: You're right, Ma. Job hunting is hard work.

MRS. VARNEY (LIVE FROM OFFSTAGE): Just remember, with your own job, you could get your own place, and I'll get my sewing room back. You've been living in the rec room for five years!

DENNY: I get it, Ma, I get it.

MRS. VARNEY (LIVE FROM OFFSTAGE) *(mimicking Denny's same rhythm)*: But you don't, Denny, you don't. Get a job!

DENNY mimics Mrs. Varney mouth with his hands, for Eugene's benefit.

DENNY *(sotto voce)*: Get a job...!

MRS. VARNEY (LIVE FROM OFFSTAGE): Now, I just came in to tell you that your church friend Walter is here. I'll send him down with sandwiches.

EUGENE: Thank you!

MRS. VARNEY exits, leaving the door open.

DENNY: This is boss! We'll sing for Wally and he can tell me what you're doing wrong.

EUGENE: Oh that'll be helpful. Church people are good at being judgy.

> *WALLY enters, kicks the door shut behind him, and comes down the stairs. He is carrying a tray loaded with sandwiches and small cartons of milk with straws. He has a newspaper section folded under his arm.*

WALLY: Wally Wally Oxen Free!

DENNY: You're it.

> *DENNY tags Eugene.*

EUGENE: Ow!

DENNY: Hey Wally.

EUGENE: Hey Wally.

WALLY: Hey is for horses. *(Holding out the tray)* And sandwiches are for lunch.

> *EUGENE grabs the tray and takes it to the counter.*

EUGENE: Thank golly. Denny was trying to starve me.

> *EUGENE begins to eat.*

WALLY: What's buzzin', cuzzin'?

DENNY: Job hunting.

EUGENE: Like usual.

WALLY: Don't I know it.

DENNY & EUGENE *(together, to Wally)*: If you know it, you owe it.

> *DENNY slugs Wally in the arm.*

DENNY: Now watch us, Wally.

#1B: "SH-BOOM: PART 3"

Maybe you can tell me what's wrong with Eugene.

> *DENNY pulls EUGENE over to practice again. EUGENE begins with sandwich in hand.*

(Singing)
LIFE COULD BE A DREAM

EUGENE *(mouthful of sandwich)*:
SH-BOOM, SH-BOOM

> *DENNY grabs sandwich from EUGENE and puts it down on the tray.*

DENNY:
IF I COULD TAKE YOU UP TO PARADISE UP ABOVE

EUGENE:
  SH-BOOM, SH-BOOM
DENNY:
  IF YOU WOULD TELL ME I'M THE ONLY ONE THAT YOU LOVE
EUGENE:
  SH-BOOM, SH-BOOM
DENNY:
  LIFE COULD BE A DREAM SWEETHEART

WALLY: Hey— can I sing too?

EUGENE: Sure. Follow me.

DENNY: No. Follow me!

> *WALLY puts down the newspaper and joins in, with EUGENE*
> *giving him instructions.*

DENNY, EUGENE & WALLY:
  LIFE COULD BE A DREAM
  IF ONLY ALL OUR PRECIOUS PLANS WOULD COME TRUE
  IF YOU WOULD LET ME SPEND MY WHOLE LIFE LOVING YOU
  LIFE COULD BE A DREAM, SWEETHEART
  SH-BOOM, SH-BOOM
  DEE-OO-EE-OO, SH-BOOM, SH-BOOM
  DEE-OO-EE-OO, SH-BOOM, SH-BOOM
  SWEETHEART!
  SH-BOOM!

> *Button for Applause.*

WALLY: Hey— that was neato! Are you getting a singing job?

EUGENE: No job. It's for the radio contest.

WALLY: Sounds like a lot of fun.

DENNY: Don't get any big ideas, loser-doozer. It's really hip to be in a twosome right now, and that's just Eugene and me.

WALLY *(correcting Denny's grammar)*: Eugene and I.

DENNY: No, Eugene and me.

EUGENE: Yeah. Eugene and me.

WALLY: Don't get your tighty-whities in a veggie-wedgie. I just came by for sandwiches.

> *WALLY hands DENNY a note that was on the tray.*

Oh! I almost forgot. This is for you.

> *DENNY grabs note. EUGENE reads over DENNY's shoulder.*

EUGENE: It's an eviction notice!

DENNY: In my Mom's handwriting.

> *DENNY crumples the note and tosses it.*
>
> *WALLY picks up the newspaper he brought in.*

WALLY: She sent down this message too.

> *WALLY holds the newspaper out in front of DENNY.*

#2: "GET A JOB"

> *(Cont'd; singing)*
> YIP YIP YIP YIP YIP
> GET A JOB

DENNY: Oh great!

EUGENE:
> GET A JOB

DENNY: You too, Eugene?

WALLY:
> JUST A JOB

WALLY & EUGENE:
> SHA DA DA DA, SHA DA DA DA DA

WALLY:
> ANY JOB

WALLY & EUGENE:
> JUST A JOB, BOY, TRY AND GET A JOB

WALLY:
> YIP YIP YIP YIP YIP YIP YIP YIP

WALLY & EUGENE:
> MUM MUM MUM MUM MUM MUM

WALLY:
> GET A JOB

WALLY & EUGENE:
> SHA DA DA DA, SHA DA DA DA DA

DENNY:	**WALLY & EUGENE:**
EVERY DAY ABOUT THIS TIME	
SHE STARTS A-CRYIN' THAT I OUGHTA	
GET A JOB	SHA DA DA DA,
	SHA DA DA DA DA
AFTER BREAKFAST EVERYDAY	
SHE THROWS THE WANT ADS IN MY WAY	
AND SHE NEVER FAILS TO SAY	

> *WALLY imitates Mrs. Varney by putting on her robe and head scarf from the laundry basket.*

WALLY:	DENNY & EUGENE:
GET A JOB	SHA DA DA DA, SHA DA DA DA DA
TRY TO GET A JOB	SHA DA DA DA, SHA DA DA DA DA
JUST A JOB	SHA DA DA DA, SHA DA DA DA DA
A BIG FAT JOB!	JUST A JOB, BOY

WALLY & EUGENE:
TRY AND GET A JOB!
YIP YIP YIP YIP YIP YIP YIP YIP
MUM MUM MUM MUM MUM MUM

WALLY:
GET A JOB

DENNY wants to have fun instead of getting nagged at.

DENNY: Hey— basement band!

EUGENE gets a badminton racket for a guitar.

EUGENE: I call guitar!

DENNY grabs a bowling trophy for a saxophone.

DENNY: I call saxophone!

WALLY grabs the broom to become an upright bass.

WALLY: I call broom bass!

THEY all play their instruments, making a cacophony of musical noise.

DENNY:	WALLY & EUGENE:
AND WHEN I GET THE PAPER	DIP DA DOO DOO DIP DA DOO DOO
I READ IT THROUGH AND THROUGH	DIP DA DOO DOO DIP DA DOO DOO
AND MAMA NEVER FAILS TO SAY	DIP DA DOO DOO DIP DA DOO DOO

WALLY & EUGENE:
IF THERE IS ANY WORK FOR YOU

DENNY:
AND WHEN I GO BACK TO THE HOUSE
I HEAR MY MAMA'S MOUTH
PREACHING AND A-CRYING
TELLIN' ME THAT I'M LYING 'BOUT A JOB

MRS. VARNEY opens the door and enters.

LIGHTS: Lights flashing.

MRS. VARNEY (LIVE FROM OFFSTAGE):
THAT YOU NEVER COULD FIND
TRY TO GET A JOB!

> **LIGHTS:** *Lights flashing, more intense*
> *(on the word "Job").*

LIKE YOUR FRIENDS EUGENE AND WALTER
THEY'VE GOT VERY NICE JOBS!

> **LIGHTS:** *Lights flashing, even more*
> *intense (on the word "Jobs").*

YIP YIP YIP YIP YIP YIP YIP YIP
MUM MUM MUM MUM MUM MUM
MRS. VARNEY & DENNY:
YIP YIP YIP YIP YIP YIP YIP YIP
MUM MUM MUM MUM MUM MUM
MRS. VARNEY, WALLY & EUGENE:
YIP YIP YIP YIP YIP YIP YIP YIP
MUM MUM MUM MUM MUM MUM
MRS. VARNEY (LIVE FROM OFFSTAGE):
GET A JOB!
DENNY, EUGENE & WALLY:
SHA DA DA DA DA

> *Button for Applause.*

> *EUGENE and WALLY each grab a sandwich.*

DENNY: Thanks for taking her side, spaz-heads.

> *EUGENE & WALLY shrug, then begin to eat.*

MRS. VARNEY (LIVE FROM OFFSTAGE): Now how are those sandwiches?

WALLY: Super-good, Mrs. V! Just like always.

MRS. VARNEY (LIVE FROM OFFSTAGE): Oh Walter, you're such a good boy. Please give my regards to your father, the Father.

WALLY: You betcha, Mrs. V!

MRS. VARNEY (LIVE FROM OFFSTAGE) *(exiting):* Bye, bye, boys.

> *DENNY reaches up and slams the door.*

DENNY *(to Wally):* What are you, best friends with my mom now?

WALLY *(picking up a sandwich):* No doubt! Your mother makes the best peanut butter and banana sandwiches this side of the Mississippi.

> *EUGENE and DENNY turn to each other and spell it out fast—*
> *a childhood game they've played before.*

DENNY & EUGENE: Mississippi! M-I-Double-S-I-Double-S-I-Double P-I.

DENNY finishes first and slugs EUGENE in the arm.

EUGENE *(with a peanut-butter mouthful)*: Not fair. I have peanut butter in my mouth!

WALLY: You should listen to your mother, Denny.

EUGENE: Yeah. Mothers are always right.

DENNY: Oh yeah? She keeps buggin' me about a job. I don't need a job.

EUGENE & WALLY *(together)*: Yeah you do.

WALLY: What if she kicks you out? You'll be super-sorry.

DENNY: She'll be super-sorry! I'm gonna win that contest, and then I can live anywhere I want.

WALLY: So what's up with this contest?

DENNY: Don't you pay attention to anything? It's all over the radio.

WALLY: Sor— ry. At our house we only listen to church music and junk like that.

DENNY: Here's the dealio. We're gonna win a huge singing contest with Whopper Radio and "Bullseye" Miller.

EUGENE & DENNY sing the Big Whopper Radio jingle.

#2A: BIG WHOPPER RADIO JINGLE

DENNY & EUGENE:
BIG WHOPPER RADIO!

THEY quickly make the bullseye noise with bow-and-arrow gestures.

WALLY: "Bullseye" Miller? Oh, he's super-duper nice.

DENNY: You say it like you know him.

WALLY: I do know him.

DENNY and EUGENE move in.

DENNY: You know "Bullseye" Miller?

EUGENE: From the radio?

WALLY: Of course I do. I see him at church every Sunday. He sits in the back. *(Conspiratorially)* With the Democrats.

DENNY & EUGENE: Ohhhhhhh.

WALLY: "Bullseye" is also the Caller at Monday Night Bingo.

EUGENE: That's tonight!

WALLY: Bingo!

WALLY & EUGENE laugh at Wally's joke.

DENNY: Wally— could you go tonight and put in a good word? It might help us win the contest.

WALLY: Sure. Can I sing in the contest too?

DENNY: I dunno, Wally. This is very different from high school and the Crooning Crab Cakes.

EUGENE: Yeah. We have to sing and dance at the same time. It's hard.

WALLY: I'm more than just a Crab Cake. I sing in the church choir now.

DENNY: Sorry, Wally. This is the real world.

EUGENE: Yeah. The real world.

DENNY: So later, gator.

EUGENE: In a while, crocodile.

WALLY: Oh yeah? Maybe I'll just go home and get ready for Monday Night Bingo. *(Takes a step away, then turns back)* Which happens to be tonight. *(Takes a step away, then turns back)* In the real world. *(Takes a step away, then turns back)* With my good friend "Bullseye" Miller.

> *WALLY makes the 'arrow-in-the-bullseye' gesture with a tiny noise and makes a big show as if to leave. HE dramatically slows his exit on the steps and listens.*

DENNY: Hold on— group meeting.

> *DENNY pulls Eugene over away from Wally.*

(To Eugene)

Whattaya think, little buddy?

> *DENNY & EUGENE look over at WALLY, who looks away.*

EUGENE: Well, if Wally joins, I won't be the only one in the back row.

> *DENNY points to EUGENE, who points right back, followed by a ritualized thumbs-up gesture. This happens quickly and should look like something they've done numerous times before.*

DENNY: Good point.

> *DENNY crosses to the steps, and WALLY crosses back down.*

Guess what, Wally? Twosomes are out and threesomes are in. Can you sing something for me?

WALLY: Sure. Here's something from church choir:

> *WALLY sings reverently.*

#2B: CHOIR OF ANGELS

(Cont'd; singing)
ANGELS UP ON HIGH

EUGENE: Wait a minute, Wally. I sing very high, so you have to sing down low.

> *WALLY sings a similar phrase ending an octave lower.*

WALLY:
    ANGELS DOWN BELOW

DENNY: Can you blend in?

WALLY *(proudly)*: I do every day.

EUGENE: Say yes, say yes, say yes, say yes...

DENNY: Okay, you're in.

> *WALLY and DENNY offer hands to shake on it.*

> *DENNY pulls up at the last minute, pointing at WALLY. WALLY's hand stays in place.*

On a trial basis.

> *DENNY places his hand forward to shake.*

> *WALLY pulls his hand up. DENNY keeps his hand out.*

WALLY: Not so fast. What'll it cost me?

EUGENE *(leaning in to Wally)*: Only your dignity.

> *WALLY thinks for a quick moment, then enthusiastically:*

WALLY: Okay, I'm in.

> *WALLY and DENNY shake on it.*

EUGENE: Yay for us! *(To Wally)* Now, we have to sing in the background because Denny won't let anyone else sing lead, *(Toward Denny)* ...even though I got straight A's in Mr. Lee's choir class three years in a row!!

DENNY: Cool your jet, teacher's pet. It's my group, so follow the leader.

EUGENE *(to Wally)*: I just think everyone deserves a chance to sing out front.

DENNY: Now we need a new name for the group. It was Denny's Dynamic Duo, but that won't work anymore.

EUGENE: Duo means two.

DENNY: We need something that'll make us stand out in a crowd.

WALLY *(raising his hand as if in class)*: Oh! Oh! Oh! Oh! I have an idea.

> *DENNY 'calls' on WALLY by pointing to him.*

How about "The Singing Saints?"

DENNY: No, no— too churchy.

WALLY: Okay. How about... "The Heavenly Hummers?"

DENNY: That's even churchier. Skip the name for now.

EUGENE: Skip the name for now.

DENNY: What we really need is fifty dollars.

EUGENE: What we really need is... Fifty Dollars? For what?

DENNY: It's the entrance fee for the contest. Everyone's gotta have it.

EUGENE: Denny, you didn't tell me about fifty dollars!

DENNY: It slipped my mind.

EUGENE: That's a huge thing to slip your mind. Where are we going to get fifty dollars?

> *THEY both look to WALLY.*

DENNY: Wally...?

WALLY: Not even a fin. I only get minimum wage down at the Piggly Wiggly.

DENNY: Shoot.

WALLY: Double shoot.

EUGENE & WALLY (*quickly to each other*): Triple shoot!

> *Playing a childhood game, THEY finger shoot at each other, elaborately re-enacting an old western shoot-out. EUGENE always "dies" in their imagined spaghetti western.*

DENNY: Cut the gas, fellas. We'll just have to find someone to give us the money. What we need is a sponsor!

EUGENE: Oh! Like my mother. She has a sponsor.

DENNY: No—not that kind of sponsor. More like what they have on television.

WALLY: Just like Monday Night Bingo. Their sponsor is Big Stuff Auto.

DENNY: Would Big Stuff Auto sponsor us?

WALLY: Could be. "Big" Earl Franklin owns Big Stuff— he was a Crooning Crab Cake back in the day at Springfield High.

DENNY: Go Chipmunks!

WALLY & EUGENE: Go Chipmunks!

> *THEY ALL make chipmunk faces first to each other, then out.*

WALLY: "Big" Earl and his daughter Lois both sing in the church choir. You remember her— she was a song leader at Springfield High. Heavenly voice.

EUGENE: Are you talking about Lois Franklin from Springfield High Lois Franklin?

WALLY: One and the same.

EUGENE: You mean Lois Franklin who broke my heart into a zillion pieces Lois Franklin?

DENNY: Hold on, Eugene...

EUGENE: She crushed me! I asked her out to the school carnival, and she turned me down.

> *EUGENE grabs WALLY by the shirt collar, threateningly.*

She turned me down!!!!

> *DENNY grabs EUGENE and pulls him away.*

DENNY: It's time to move on, Eugene. That was the fifth grade.

WALLY: Well she seemed super sweet to me. *(Whispering to Denny)* Last week at choir practice I tripped over a pew, and she helped me up. She has a very soft touch.

EUGENE: Watch out— she'll crush you!

DENNY: Wally, can you get "Big" Earl to come watch us sing tomorrow?

WALLY: No doubt. I'll drop by his place right after work.

EUGENE: I dunno, Denny. I'm getting a bad feeling about this. Maybe you should just get a regular job.

DENNY: What would I do with a regular job? I'm a dreamer, Eugene. The world needs dreamers.

WALLY: Hey— how's that for a name? *(Painting a picture out front)* The Dreamers!

DENNY *(unimpressed)*: The Dreamers?

> *EUGENE whispers in WALLY's ear.*

WALLY *(correcting himself, painting a picture again)*: Denny and the Dreamers.

DENNY: Hey— I like it! Denny and the Dreamers!!

> *WALLY and EUGENE jump up and down in celebration, chanting together.*

WALLY & EUGENE: Denny and the Dreamers! Denny and the Dreamers! Denny and the Dreamers!!!

> *THEY yell and scream with excitement.*

> *MRS. VARNEY opens the door and enters.*

LIGHTS: Lights flashing.

MRS. VARNEY (LIVE FROM OFFSTAGE): Denny! Cut out that racket!!

EUGENE *(crossing to landing)*: Sorry, Mrs. Varney. We just got super-excited for the singing contest.

MRS. VARNEY (LIVE FROM OFFSTAGE): The singing contest?

DENNY: Eugene!!

> *DENNY shoots an angry look at EUGENE, who silently apologizes.*

MRS. VARNEY (LIVE FROM OFFSTAGE): Dennis Lloyd Varney, you know I don't allow rocking and rolling in this household.

> *DENNY once again makes annoyed "talking noises" with his hands toward his mother.*

When are you going to grow up and find a vocation?

DENNY: A vacation? I'd love a vacation. Where are we going?

EUGENE and WALLY crack up, trying to not let her hear.

MRS. VARNEY (LIVE FROM OFFSTAGE): I said VO-cation. You know, like a job!!

DENNY: It's okay, Ma. Eugene's Dad just hired me down at the soda fountain. I start tomorrow.

EUGENE: Hey!

DENNY shoots EUGENE a look.

MRS. VARNEY (LIVE FROM OFFSTAGE): Is that right Eugene? Is my boy telling the truth?

EUGENE *(pleadingly to Denny, afraid to lie)*: Denny...!

DENNY *(conspiratorially)*: Do this for me and I'll let you sing lead for "Big" Earl tomorrow.

MRS. VARNEY (LIVE FROM OFFSTAGE) *(untrusting, drawn out)*: Eugene...?

EUGENE *(to Mrs. Varney, holding up crossed fingers behind his back)*: Absolutely, Mrs. Varney. Abso-tiv'n-lutely.

EUGENE and DENNY shakes hands.

MRS. VARNEY (LIVE FROM OFFSTAGE): Oh that's wonderful. Now that you're a working man, you can stop all of these noisy rock and roll shenanigans.

DENNY: That's right, Ma. No more shenanigans for me. As a matter of fact, it's time for my big boy nap!

DENNY slams the door on Mama.

#3: MAMA DON'T ALLOW IT

I'm gonna be the next big thing in rock 'n' roll. Mama won't know what hit her!

> *(Singing)*
> MAMA DON'T ALLOW NO ROCK 'N ROLL IN HERE

EUGENE & WALLY:
> ROCK 'N ROLL IN HERE

DENNY:
> MAMA DON'T ALLOW NO ROCK 'N ROLL IN HERE

EUGENE & WALLY:
> ROCK 'N ROLL IN HERE

DENNY:
> I DON'T CARE WHAT MAMA DON'T ALLOW
> GONNA ROCK 'N ROLL ANY-OLD-HOW
> MAMA DON'T ALLOW NO ROCK 'N ROLL IN HERE

EUGENE & WALLY:
> ROCK 'N ROLL IN HERE

DENNY, EUGENE & WALLY:
NO MAMA DON'T ALLOW IT
NO MAMA DON'T ALLOW IT
DENNY:
MAMA DON'T ALLOW NO DOO-WAH SINGIN' IN HERE
EUGENE & WALLY:
DOO-WAH, DOO-WAH, DOO-WAH
DENNY:
OH, MAMA DON'T ALLOW NO BOP-BOP SINGIN' IN HERE
EUGENE & WALLY:
BOP, BOP
DENNY, EUGENE & WALLY:
BOP, SHOO-WAH
EUGENE:
YOUR MAMA HAS A HEART THAT NEVER MELTS
WALLY:
WE'RE GONNA DOO-WAH DIDDY, DIDDY SOMEWHERE ELSE
DENNY:
MAMA DON'T ALLOW NO DOO-WAH SINGIN' IN HERE
DENNY, EUGENE & WALLY:
DOOBIE DOO-WAH, SHOOP DOO-WAH

> *DENNY picks up a referee's whistle from behind the bar. He places the whistle around his neck.*

DENNY, EUGENE & WALLY:
NO MAMA DON'T ALLOW IT
NO MAMA DON'T ALLOW IT
DENNY:
MAMA DON'T ALLOW NO MASHED POTATO IN HERE

> *DENNY does the 'Mashed Potato' dance, followed by the others.*

EUGENE & WALLY:
IT'S MASHED POTATO TIME
DENNY:
MAMA DON'T ALLOW NO WAH WATUSI IN HERE

> *DENNY does the 'Wah Watusi' dance, followed by the others.*

EUGENE & WALLY:
DOO-DOO, DO THE WAH WATUSI
DENNY:
I DON'T CARE WHAT MAMA DON'T ALLOW

> *THEY combine the two dance steps.*

DENNY, EUGENE & WALLY:
    WE'RE GONNA MASH AND WATUSI
    ANY-OLD-HOW

*   EUGENE and WALLY cross to get a golf club and the broom.*

DENNY:
    MAMA DON'T ALLOW NO

*   DENNY blows on the referee's whistle toward the door.*

    IN HERE

*   EUGENE and WALLY answer with loud banging on the radiator and posts.*

*   MRS. VARNEY opens the door and enters.*

LIGHTS: Lights flashing.

MRS. VARNEY (LIVE FROM OFFSTAGE): Dennis!! What's that noise?!

*   DENNY runs to the bell by the bar and begins clanging the bell.*

DENNY, EUGENE & WALLY:
    NO MAMA DON'T ALLOW IT

MRS. VARNEY (LIVE FROM OFFSTAGE): Dennis! Keep it down!

DENNY, EUGENE & WALLY:
    NO MAMA DON'T ALLOW IT

MRS. VARNEY (LIVE FROM OFFSTAGE): Dennis!!!

DENNY:
    MAMA DON'T ALLOW NO
    ROCK 'N ROLL IN HERE

MRS. VARNEY (LIVE FROM OFFSTAGE): Dennis! Stop that racket!

EUGENE & WALLY:
    ROCK 'N ROLL IN HERE

DENNY:
    OH, MAMA DON'T ALLOW NO DOO WAH DIDDY IN HERE

LIGHTS: Lights flashing.

*   MRS. VARNEY flashes the lights repeatedly. <u>SHE continues to ad lib throughout the rest of the song.</u>*

MRS. VARNEY (LIVE FROM OFFSTAGE) *(ad-libbed through the following):* Your grandmother told me this would happen. She always said that you were a rotten egg and would defy authority, and now it seems to have come true. I ask nicely until I'm blue in the face, and yet you insist on embarrassing me in front of the entire neighborhood. (etc.)

EUGENE & WALLY:
OODY WADDY, RAMA LAMA DING DONG
DENNY:
I DON'T CARE WHAT MAMA DON'T ALLOW
I'M GONNA WIN THAT CONTEST ANY-OLD-HOW
MAMA DON'T ALLOW NO

> *DENNY clangs the bell by the bar three times.*

IN HERE

> *THEY run around banging on the furniture and walls, DENNY blowing the whistle, while MRS. VARNEY speaks throughout.*

> *[Note: It helps if DENNY blows the whistle to the beat of the music, every other beat, to keep everyone in time with the music for the end.]*

MRS. VARNEY (LIVE FROM OFFSTAGE): Keep down that racket, young man. Are you intentionally disobeying me?! I spared the rod and spoiled the child, there's certainly no doubt about it!

DENNY, EUGENE & WALLY:
NO MAMA DON'T ALLOW IT
EUGENE & WALLY:
ZIP ZIP
MRS. VARNEY (LIVE FROM OFFSTAGE) *(shouted):*
GET A JOB!

> *Blackout.*

> *[MRS. VARNEY should leave door open for DENNY to exit for quick change and make his first entrance in the next scene.]*

#3A: MAMA DON'T ALLOW IT PLAYOFF

ACT I, SCENE 2

THE FOLLOWING EVENING: TUESDAY.

> *SOUND: In the dark we hear the radio over the music playoff from the previous scene:*

DISC JOCKEY (V.O.): Hey cool cats! This is "Bullseye" Miller!

> *SOUND: "Arrow hitting a bullseye" sound effect.*

Everybody's goin' ape for Saturday night's big Whopper Radio Rock 'n' Roll Round-up!

> *SOUND: Radio Jingle: "Big Whopper Radio."*

Tickets are on sale now at Fancy Miss Nancy's School of Dancy, where Fancy Nancy says, "If you can't dance by closing time, your next lesson is freeeeeee!" And for all of you croonin' cats out there: Sign up today for the "Dream of a Lifetime" Talent Search. It's the most exciting thing to hit this town since the opening of the Wonder Bread factory. Don't just scheme— "Life Could Be A Dream!"

> *LIGHTS up.*

> *There is a new tray of snacks on the table. WALLY and EUGENE are practicing dance moves using badminton rackets as microphones.*

> *DENNY enters, shuts the door and races down the steps.*

DENNY: No sign of him yet, Wally. Are you sure he said tonight?

WALLY: No doubt. Right after closing is what he said.

EUGENE: And why do we have to audition? It makes me so nervous to always be judged by everyone. Why can't he just give us the money? We were Crooning Crab Cakes too, ya know.

> *EUGENE crosses and looks up the stairs, nervous.*

WALLY *(whispering)*: Denny, why are you letting Eugene sing lead? He seems super-duper nervous.

DENNY *(whispering)*: It's your fault. You got my mom all worked up about a job, so I had to improvise. Don't worry— it'll only be this one time.

WALLY *(whispering)*: I just hope he can handle it.

EUGENE *(nervously)*: When's he gonna get here? When's he gonna get here?!

DENNY: Cool your beans, little buddy. Everything is gonna be fine.

WALLY: Mind over matter, Eugene. Mind over matter.

EUGENE: Mind over matter. Mind over matter.

EUGENE crosses away, muttering the mantra to himself.

DENNY tosses a towel to WALLY.

DENNY: And don't let "Big" Earl see you sweat, Wally. He'll think we're all loser-doozers.

WALLY: Oh. Not to worry. "Big" Earl's not actually coming— he's sending over his head mechanic to check us out.

DENNY: A mechanic?

WALLY: Head mechanic.

EUGENE: A head mechanic? What's a head mechanic?

DENNY: Something you need but can't afford.

EUGENE: Ha ha. You're rubber, I'm glue. Everything you say bounces of you and sticks to...

HE thinks.

Wait, that doesn't work...

WALLY: Don't worry, I met the guy. He seemed super-duper swell-and-a-half.

MRS. VARNEY opens the door and enters.

LIGHTS: Lights flashing.

MRS. VARNEY (LIVE FROM OFFSTAGE): Denny. Your new friend is up here.

EUGENE panics, and WALLY helps calm him down with his 'mind over matter' mantra.

DENNY: Send him down, Ma.

MRS. VARNEY (LIVE FROM OFFSTAGE): Denny— if your new job at the Sweet Shoppe doesn't work out, maybe you could ask this young man for a job. It looks like he actually works for a living.

DENNY *(with accompanying hand gestures)*: Naggedy-nag, goodbye.

DENNY shuts the door in her face.

Now hurry up— get in line. And whatever you do, don't goof it all up.

THEY line up: DENNY next to the steps, WALLY in the middle and EUGENE on the end.

EUGENE: A-ten-hut!

DENNY, EUGENE and WALLY stand at attention.

DUKE enters, leaving the door open. DUKE is wearing jeans and a work shirt, with "Big Stuff Auto" on the back, and his name over the chest pocket. HE has touches of grease smeared on his arms and face.

DUKE crosses down next to DENNY.

DUKE: Hey fellas. I'm Duke. From Big Stuff Auto.

DENNY (*thrusting out his hand*): I'm Denny. From Denny and the Dreamers.

> *DUKE shakes his hand. DENNY pretends that DUKE's grip is way too hard.*

> (*Play acting*)

Oh, oh... oh!

> *DENNY pulls his hand away.*

As my mom would say, that's quite a grip.

> *He playfully slugs DUKE in the arm and crosses to DUKE's other side.*

> *DUKE moves down the line to meet them one by one.*

WALLY: Hi Duke. Remember me from yesterday?

> *WALLY puts out his hand to shake.*

DUKE: Sure. With the sweaty palms.

> *WALLY wipes his hand on the towel/his pants, and then DUKE shakes his hand.*

Nice to see you again.

> *WALLY crosses to the other side of EUGENE.*

> *EUGENE is staring awkwardly at DUKE.*

WALLY: This is Eugene. (*Leaning in toward Eugene, whispering*) Shake hands.

> *EUGENE grasps DUKE's forearm in a vice-like grip.*

EUGENE: Please don't judge me.

> *WALLY pulls EUGENE away toward DENNY. DUKE crosses right and turns back to the boys.*

DUKE: Nice to meet all of you,.

> *MRS. VARNEY enters (door is open).*

LIGHTS: Lights flashing.

MRS. VARNEY (LIVE FROM OFFSTAGE): Denny, I'm off to work the late shift at the diner. But you've got another friend up here. This one is a girl.

> *DENNY, EUGENE & WALLY look at each other and shrug.*

DENNY: I don't know any girls.

MRS. VARNEY (LIVE FROM OFFSTAGE): Mind your manners and treat her like a lady. I'll send her right down.

> *MRS. VARNEY exits, leaving door open.*

DUKE: That must be "Big" Earl's daughter, Lois.

EUGENE (*panicked*): What?!

DUKE: He said he wanted a woman's point-of-view as well.

EUGENE: Disaster! Disaster! *(To Denny)* I can't sing in front of her!

DENNY: Just pretend that you don't know her!

EUGENE *(panicked, inconsolable)*: But I do know her! I do know her!

DENNY & WALLY: Sssshhhhh!

> *LOIS enters and closes the door. SHE starts down the steps. SHE wears a distinctive scarf.*
>
> *DENNY & WALLY line up at the stairs, EUGENE at the far end of the bar, hiding.*
>
> *DUKE moves to the other side of the room.*

LOIS: Hello, boys. I'm Lois Franklin.

> *DENNY tries to be cool, overly suave, taking her hand.*

DENNY *(in a slightly adenoidal high-pitched voice)*: I'm Denny. *(Clearing his throat, repeats in deeper voice)* I'm Denny. From Denny & the Dreamers.

> *WALLY awkwardly thrusts his hand out toward her.*

WALLY: And I'm Wally. From the choir at church. Remember the pew?

> *HE quickly illustrates her helping him up.*

LOIS *(shaking his hand)*: Oh yes! It's nice to see you again.

> *WALLY holds onto her hand, pulling it close to his face.*

WALLY: So soft.

> *LOIS pulls her hand away, wiping it on her dress.*

DENNY: And this...

> *DENNY knocks on the top of the bar.*

...is Eugene.

> *EUGENE pops up from behind the bar, still clutching his badminton racket.*

LOIS: Hello.

> *EUGENE opens his mouth, finding that his tongue doesn't work. HE tries to say "I love you" but it sounds as if his tongue is three sizes too big.*

EUGENE: [unintelligible words]

> *EUGENE holds the racket up in front of his face and hides back behind the bar.*
>
> *LOIS turns to DUKE.*

LOIS: And you... *(Pointing at his name badge)* ...are Duke.

DUKE: Yes. Duke Henderson.

LOIS: I'm "Big" Earl's daughter, Lois.

THEY shake hands.

DUKE: Nice to finally meet you, Miss Franklin.

LOIS: I'm sorry we haven't met before now. I help out in the front office, but Daddy never lets me go back into the garage. He runs a pretty tight ship.

DUKE: You're telling me!

LOIS: In fact, he has an absolute rule against me talking to any of the men in the shop.

LOIS leans in, conspiratorially.

You know— wrong side of the tracks and all.

DUKE *(taken aback)*: Oh. Of course.

LOIS *(playfully)*: Just kidding, Duke. Loosen up.

DUKE: Sure, Miss Franklin.

LOIS turns her attention to the boys.

LOIS: Okay, boys— down to business. Big Stuff Auto is opening three new shops around the state next month, so now is the perfect time to attach our name to something really big. "Big" Earl— that's Daddy— said he would sponsor a singing group only if they had a real shot at winning the big contest. Are you boys up to the task?

DENNY: Ready and willing!

WALLY: No doubt!

EUGENE: [Loud unintelligible whimper!]

LOIS: Daddy is looking for a good, sound investment, so let's see what you've got.

DENNY: One good, sound investment coming up!

DENNY points to the stools and DUKE leads LOIS over to sit. DENNY grabs a badminton racket.

EUGENE: But, but, but, but, but, but, but...

WALLY *(whispering to Eugene)*: Mind over matter, Eugene.

EUGENE *(repeating to himself)*: Mind over matter, mind over matter, mind over matter...

WALLY grabs a badminton racket for himself, and gives EUGENE a tennis racket.

DENNY *(to Lois and Duke)*: This may seem a little rough— we're just getting started. We'll be 18 karat by Saturday. *(To Eugene)* Just like we practiced, alright?

EUGENE grunts, distracted.

THEY use the rackets as microphones.

#4: TEARS ON MY PILLOW

DENNY, EUGENE & WALLY:
OOOOH, OOOOH
OOOOH, OOOOH

EUGENE:	**DENNY & WALLY:**
YOU DON'T REMEMBER ME	OOH
BUT I REMEMBER YOU	OOH
IT WAS NOT SO LONG AGO	OOH
YOU BROKE MY HEART IN TWO	OOH
TEARS ON MY PILLOW	OOH WAH
PAIN IN MY HEART	OOH WAH

EUGENE gestures toward LOIS.

EUGENE:
CAUSED BY YOU

DENNY & WALLY:
YOU!

EUGENE:	**DENNY & WALLY:**
IF WE COULD START ANEW	OOH
I WOULDN'T HESITATE	OOH
I'D GLADLY TAKE YOU BACK	OOH
AND TEMPT THE HAND OF FATE	OOH
TEARS ON MY PILLOW	OOH WAH
PAIN IN MY HEART	OOH WAH
CAUSED BY	

DENNY, EUGENE & WALLY:
YOU

EUGENE starts to break down, and WALLY pulls him back. WALLY consoles EUGENE as DENNY rushes forward to try to salvage the song.

DENNY:
LOVE IS NOT A GADGET
LOVE IS NOT A TOY
WHEN YOU FIND THE ONE YOU LOVE
SHE'LL FILL YOUR HEART WITH JOY

EUGENE rushes forward to finish the song with renewed energy, pushing DENNY aside.

EUGENE:	**DENNY & WALLY:**
BEFORE YOU GO AWAY	OOH
MY DARLING, THINK OF ME	OOH
THERE STILL MAY BE A CHANCE	OOH

EUGENE (CONT'D):	DENNY & WALLY (CONT'D):
TO END MY MISERY	OOH
TEARS ON MY PILLOW	OOH WAH
PAIN IN MY HEART	OOH WAH

> *EUGENE accusingly points at LOIS again. HE breaks down during the last part of the song.*

CAUSED BY YOU

DENNY & WALLY:
YOU

EUGENE:
WHOA

DENNY & WALLY:
YOU

EUGENE:
WHOA—

DENNY & WALLY:
YOU

> *EUGENE sings a final falsetto phrase.*

EUGENE:
YOU!

> *EUGENE ends the song at LOIS' feet.*
>
> *Button for Applause.*
>
> *The BOYS gather together as DUKE and LOIS quietly confer.*

WALLY *(whispering to Denny)*: Whattaya think? How'd we do?

DENNY *(referring to Eugene)*: This loser-doozer ruined everything!

EUGENE *(to Denny)*: I'm sorry. *(To Wally)* I'm sorry.

WALLY *(to Eugene)*: What happened to mind over matter?

EUGENE: It only doesn't matter if you really don't mind!

> *DUKE and LOIS cross in.*

LOIS: Fellas— that wasn't half bad.

> *The boys are happily surprised.*

DENNY: I knew it! *(To Wally)* Told ya so.

LOIS: Everything was pretty good, until your lead singer broke down.

EUGENE: Eugene! My name is Eugene!

DENNY: Don't worry. He's usually in the back row.

EUGENE *(to himself)*: Loser-doozer...!

LOIS: With just one more little change, I think Daddy will sponsor you.

DENNY: You name it, we'll change it.

LOIS: I know you boys were all Crooning Crab Cakes at Springfield High.

DENNY: Go Chipmunks!

DENNY, EUGENE, LOIS & WALLY: Go Chipmunks!

> *THEY all four make chipmunk faces to each other, then out.*

LOIS: Daddy was a founding member of the Crooning Crab Cakes, and they started out as a barbershop quartet. Most of the big groups today are quartets as well: The Four Freshmen, The Four Preps...

> *WALLY jumps in.*

WALLY *(painting a picture out front)*: The Four Dreamers.

> *EUGENE whispers quickly to Wally.*

> *(Correcting himself out front)*

Denny and the Four Dreamers!

LOIS: You just need one more singer to make a proper quartet.

DENNY: But we only have four days!

WALLY *(painting the same picture out front)*: Denny and the Four Days.

EUGENE: What are we gonna do?

WALLY: Say Duke— you wanna be in the group?

> *In quick *succession:*

DENNY*: Wally!

WALLY*: Well?

DUKE*: What?

EUGENE*: Wally!

WALLY *(counting them off)*: One, two, three, Duke. That makes four. *(To Lois)* And you can help us, Lois! You seem super-duper swell-and-a-half about everything.

> *DENNY and EUGENE converge on WALLY.*

DENNY: Wally— what are you doing? Follow the leader, remember?

EUGENE: Yeah, remember?

WALLY: You said you wanted to stand out in a crowd, right?

DENNY: But how do we know he can even sing?

WALLY: Of course he can sing. Look at him.

> *THEY all look at him.*

DENNY: Hey Duke— Can you sing?

DUKE: Well, a little, I guess.

WALLY *(to Denny)*: See? *(To Eugene)* See?

DENNY: Sing something for us. Just to make sure.

#4A: FALSE START

DUKE:
WELL—

WALLY (grabbing and shaking Duke's hand enthusiastically): You. Are. Hired!!

DENNY: Wait a minute, Wally. You've gotta let him get going.

WALLY: Sorry, I just got a little excited.

#5: FOOLS FALL IN LOVE

LOIS: Go ahead, Duke. Show us what you've got.

DUKE:
WELL, FOOLS FALL IN LOVE IN A HURRY
FOOLS GIVE THEIR HEARTS MUCH TOO SOON
JUST PLAY THEM TWO BARS OF "STARDUST"
JUST HANG OUT ONE SILLY MOON
OH! THEN

DUKE acknowledges the backups joining in.

	DENNY, EUGENE, WALLY:
THEY'VE GOT THEIR LOVE TORCHES BURNING	AAH
WHEN THEY SHOULD BE PLAYING IT COOL	AAH, AAH
I USED TO LAUGH BUT NOW I UNDERSTAND	AAH
SHAKE THE HAND OF A	HAND OF A
BRAND NEW FOOL	BRAND NEW FOOL
	BOP BOP BAH

DUKE joins the guys, and LOIS steps out.

LOIS:	MEN:
WELL, FOOLS FALL IN	DOOT-N-DOO-WAH
LOVE JUST LIKE	DOO DOOT DOO-WAH
SCHOOLGIRLS	DOOT-N-DOO-WAH
	DOO DOOT DOO-WAH
BLINDED BY	DOOT-N-DOO-WAH
ROSE-COLORED	DOO DOOT DOO-WAH
DREAMS	DOOT-N-DOO-WAH
	DOO DOOT DOO-WAH
THEY BUILD THEIR CASTLES	AAH—
ON WISHES	
WITH ONLY RAINBOWS	AAH—
FOR BEAMS	
OH!	OH!

LOIS (CONT'D):	MEN (CONT'D):
THEY'RE MAKING	DOOT-N-DOO-WAH
PLANS FOR THE	DOO DOOT DOO-WAH
FUTURE	DOOT-N-DOO-WAH
	DOO DOOT DOO-WAH
WHEN THEY SHOULD BE	DOOT-N-DOO-WAH
RIGHT BACK IN	DOO DOOT DOO-WAH
SCHOOL	DOOT-N-DOO-WAH
	DOO DOOT DOO-WAH
I USED TO LAUGH BUT NOW	AAH—
I UNDERSTAND	
SHAKE THE HAND OF A	HAND OF A
BRAND NEW FOOL	BRAND NEW FOOL

DUKE crosses to LOIS, the BOYS gather together and await their fate.

LOIS: Very nice.

DUKE: Miss Franklin, are you sure about this? These boys don't have much experience.

LOIS: That's why they need you to make it all work.

DUKE: What about your father?

LOIS: Leave that to me. I can convince Daddy of anything.

DUKE: Whatever you say.

LOIS: That's what I like to hear.

DENNY, EUGENE & WALLY cross over.

DENNY: So— is it a deal?

WALLY: Do we get the sponsorship?

EUGENE: Say yes, say yes, say yes, say yes...

LOIS: I think I'm looking at America's next big recording stars!

DENNY, WALLY & EUGENE celebrate, jumping up and down in excitement.

LOIS:	MEN:
OH!	OH!
THEY'RE MAKING	DOOT-N-DOO-WAH
PLANS FOR THE	DOO DOOT DOO-WAH
FUTURE	DOOT-N-DOO-WAH
	DOO DOOT DOO-WAH
WHEN THEY SHOULD BE	DOOT-N-DOO-WAH
RIGHT BACK IN	DOO DOOT DOO-WAH
SCHOOL	DOOT-N-DOO-WAH

LOIS (CONT'D):

    I USED TO LAUGH BUT NOW

    I UNDERSTAND

LOIS & DUKE:

    SHAKE THE HAND

    OF A

    BRAND

    NEW

    FOOL!

MEN (CONT'D):

    DOO DOOT DOO-WAH

    AAH—

DENNY, EUGENE & WALLY:

    COME ON AND

    SHAKE THE HAND

    WE'RE GONNA

    WIN THAT CONTEST

    AND BE COOL!

          Blackout.

#5A: FOOLS PLAYOFF

ACT I, SCENE 3

THURSDAY EVENING.

> *SOUND: In the dark we hear the radio*
> *over the music playoff from the*
> *previous scene:*

DISC JOCKEY (V.O.): Hey cool cats! This is "Bullseye" Miller!

> *SOUND: "Arrow hitting a bullseye"*
> *sound effect.*

You've got just two more days before the big Whopper Radio Rock 'n' Roll Round-up!

> *SOUND: Radio Jingle: "Big Whopper*
> *Radio."*

Tickets are on sale now at Little Betsy's Cut 'n' Curl, where Little Betsy says, "If your new hairdo becomes a hair-don't, your next Dippity Doo is freeeeeee!" And don't forget to sign up for the "Dream of a Lifetime" talent search. It'll be the biggest thing since the invention of the hula hoop! Are you America's next big recording star? Land a theme and join the team— Life Could Be A Dream!

> *Spotlight up on DUKE, wearing jeans and a white A-shirt*
> *under his work shirt. HE is singing into the end of a tennis*
> *racket, using it as a mic.*

#6: RUNAROUND SUE

DUKE:
HERE'S MY STORY, ITS SAD BUT TRUE
IT'S ABOUT A GIRL THAT I ONCE KNEW
SHE TOOK MY LOVE THEN RAN AROUND
WITH EVERY SINGLE GUY IN TOWN

> *LIGHTS up reveal DENNY, EUGENE & WALLY on the staircase.*
> *THEY step down as THEY sing, lining up behind DUKE.*
>
> *They are all rehearsing; DUKE is very smooth, with the others*
> *in varying degrees of comfort and ability.*
>
> *EUGENE is overly energetic and 'directionally challenged';*
> *WALLY is stiff without moving his hips; DENNY struggles with*
> *DUKE singing lead.*

DUKE:	**DENNY, EUGENE & WALLY:**
WHOA—	HAYP, HAYP,
	BUMDA HADY, HADY
WHOA—	HAYP, HAYP,

DUKE (CONT'D):	DENNY, EUGENE & WALLY (CONT'D):
	BUMDA HADY, HADY
WHOA—	HAYP, HAYP,
	BUMDA HADY, HADY, HAYP
	BA, BA, BA
WHOA—	HAYP, HAYP,
	BUMDA HADY, HADY
WHOA—	HAYP, HAYP,
	BUMDA HADY, HADY
WHOA—	HAYP, HAYP,
	BUMDA HADY, HADY, HAYP
	AHH—

DENNY, EUGENE and WALLY bump into each other.

THEY stop dancing and bicker during the first few lines of the verse even as THEY continue singing.

I SHOULD HAVE KNOWN IT FROM THE	HAYP, HAYP
VERY START	BUMDA HADY, HADY
THIS GIRL WOULD LEAVE ME WITH A	HAYP, HAYP
BROKEN HEART	BUMDA HADY, HADY
NOW LISTEN PEOPLE WHAT I'M	HAYP, HAYP
TELLING YOU	BUMDA HADY, HADY
A-KEEP AWAY FROM-A	HAYP
RUNAROUND SUE	
I MISS HER LIPS AND THE	HAYP, HAYP
SMILE ON HER FACE	BUMDA HADY, HADY
THE TOUCH OF MY HAND AND THIS	HAYP, HAYP
GIRL'S WARM EMBRACE	BUMDA HADY, HADY
SO IF YOU DON'T WANNA CRY	HAYP, HAYP
LIKE I DO	BUMDA HADY, HADY
A-KEEP AWAY FROM-A	HAYP
RUNAROUND SUE	

DUKE tries to help the boys as they run into each other.

WHOA, WHOA—	HAYP, HAYP,
	BUMDA HADY, HADY
WHOA—	HAYP, HAYP,
	BUMDA HADY, HADY
WHOA—	HAYP, HAYP,
	BUMDA HADY, HADY, HAYP
	AHH—

DENNY jumps front, taking the lead (and the tennis racket) from DUKE.

DENNY:	EUGENE & WALLY:
SHE LIKES TO TRAVEL AROUND	AAH, HEY
SHE'LL LOVE YOU AND SHE'LL	AAH—
PUT YOU DOWN	
NOW PEOPLE LET ME PUT YOU WISE	AAH—
SUE GOES OUT WITH OTHER GUYS	

    (To Duke)

It's Denny and the Dreamers. Not Duke and the Dreamers. Denny.

WALLY & EUGENE come forward to pull back DENNY.

EUGENE & WALLY: Denny...!

DENNY *(protesting)*: I'm not done!

    *Simultaneously:

*EUGENE: Yes you are!

*WALLY: You're done now!

EUGENE takes the tennis racket from DENNY, and passes it to DUKE.

DENNY sits and stews. During the following HE sings backup and performs the choreography halfheartedly while sitting in his chair.

DUKE:	DENNY, EUGENE & WALLY:
HERE'S THE	
MORAL AND THE STORY FROM THE	HAYP, HAYP
GUY WHO KNOWS	BUMDA HADY, HADY
I FELL IN LOVE AND MY	HAYP, HAYP
LOVE STILL GROWS	BUMDA HADY, HADY
ASK ANY FOOL THAT	HAYP, HAYP
SHE EVER KNEW, THEY'LL SAY	BUMDA HADY, HADY
A-KEEP AWAY FROM-A	HAYP
RUNAROUND SUE	
YEAH	HAYP, HAYP
STAY AWAY FROM THAT	BUMDA HADY, HADY
GIRL	HAYP, HAYP
DON'T KNOW WHAT SHE'LL DO	BUMDA HADY, HADY
NOW	HAYP, HAYP
KEEP AWAY FROM	BUMDA HADY, HADY
SUE—	HAYP, HAYP
	AAH—

DUKE, DENNY, EUGENE & WALLY:
  HAYP, HAYP!

> *DUKE moves away from the group, getting a towel.*

WALLY *(to Duke)*: So? How did we do?

DUKE: Well, fellas, I think you're all still a bit... uh... tight around the edges.

EUGENE *(muttering to himself)*: Mind over matter. Mind over matter.

DENNY: What does that even mean, tight around the edges?

DUKE: It means you know all the notes, and most of the dance moves, but you're just too stiff. You look like you're back in glee club.

DENNY: We were good in glee club.

DUKE: Glee clubs don't sell records.

DENNY: What would you know about it, head mechanic Duke?

> *DENNY pokes DUKE in his nametag when he calls him by name.*

Maybe the rest of us would look better if you didn't hog the spotlight so much.

DUKE: You fellas asked me to sing lead.

WALLY: Because you're the best at it.

DENNY: In your opinion.

WALLY: Denny. Duke is better than all Four Tops put together.

DENNY *(going off to sulk)*: It's just not right.

DUKE: Getting better is the only thing that matters right now.

EUGENE: I'm trying to get better, Duke. But I get so nervous every time I try to dance. And then I think about all of those people watching and I wonder if they'll like me after I learn to dance. And then I get all nervous again, and I dance even worse than before. And then I think about all of those people watching me dance and I just get nervouser and worser!

DUKE: We've really got to calm those nerves, Eugene. Try my secret weapon. The next time we sing, just imagine that anyone watching is in their underwear.

EUGENE: Really?

DUKE: It works like a charm.

EUGENE *(repeating to himself)*: Underwear, underwear...

> *MRS. VARNEY opens the door and enters.*

LIGHTS: *Lights flashing.*

MRS. VARNEY (LIVE FROM OFFSTAGE): Denny. That young woman is here again.

DENNY: Send her down, Ma.

> *The boys all prepare, fixing their hair, straightening clothing, etc.*

MRS. VARNEY (LIVE FROM OFFSTAGE): This is her second visit without a chaperone, Denny. It makes me wonder what goes on around here while I'm slaving away at the diner!

DENNY: We're running a brothel, Ma.

MRS. VARNEY (LIVE FROM OFFSTAGE): What? You're running a what?!

DENNY: A whorehouse! Now send her down quick, Ma, we're getting backed up!

> *DENNY slams the door.*
>
> *DENNY, WALLY and EUGENE laugh.*

DUKE: I'm glad Miss Franklin is here. It might help to get an objective viewpoint.

DENNY: Sure. Maybe she'll see that you're the one who's tight around the edges and then I'll be back in front.

> *LOIS enters, closing the door behind her. SHE comes down the stairs, looking ravishing. SHE has the same distinctive scarf.*

LOIS: Hello boys.

> *DENNY, EUGENE & WALLY rush over to greet her.*

WALLY: Gosh, Lois. You sure do look like an angel. An angel on earth.

DENNY: Let me get a chair for you.

> **Overlapping:*

*WALLY: I'll get it! Let me get the chair!

*EUGENE: I can do it, I can do it...!

> *DENNY, WALLY & EUGENE struggle over a chair.*

DENNY: Wait. Roshambo!

EUGENE & WALLY *(reverently)*: Roshambo!

> *THEY hold out their hands and begin to play 'Rock, Paper, Scissors.' THEY tie twice, then close ranks.*
>
> *After a few moments of watching the children...*

DUKE: Hello, Miss Franklin.

> *LOIS crosses to DUKE at the bar.*

LOIS: Duke, please call me Lois. Miss Franklin is so formal.

DUKE: We shouldn't get too friendly. Your father is strict. I can't afford to get on his bad side.

LOIS: Don't worry. I can handle Daddy.

DUKE: But I can't. I need this job, Miss Franklin.

LOIS: You're clearly good at what you do. You've been at the shop a year, and made head mechanic after three months. What are you worried about?

DUKE: Crossing the invisible red line.

LOIS (leaning in): What Daddy doesn't know won't hurt anyone, right?

> *THEY smolder a bit, face to face.*

> *After a beat, DUKE breaks away.*

So, how are they doing?

DUKE: Ms. Franklin, I don't think it's gonna work.

LOIS: What do you mean?

DUKE: If we're gonna win that contest, we've gotta be sharp. We've gotta be hip. We've gotta be cool.

LOIS: And...?

DUKE: Sorry to say, Miss Franklin, but if you look up uncool in the Encyclopedia, there's a picture of those boys doing that.

> *HE points to the BOYS, who are practicing a nerdy dance move.*

It's like Jerry Lewis taught The Three Stooges how to dance. It's a lost cause.

LOIS: Listen Duke, I really need to show Daddy I made the right choice with this sponsorship, so please don't give up on them yet.

DUKE: Sure. Got any ideas?

LOIS: Maybe the situation calls for some old-fashioned female persuasion.

DUKE: Whatever you say, Miss Franklin. (Playfully) Work your womanly wiles.

> *SHE moves in close to DUKE.*

LOIS: I'll even stay on my side of the red line.

> *LOIS turns to DENNY, EUGENE and WALLY.*

So boys— who's ready for some one-on-one coaching?

> **Overlapping:*

*WALLY: Me, me, me! Have some one-on-one with me!

*DENNY: I'm first. It's called Denny and the Dreamers!

*EUGENE: But I need the most help!

> *It turns into a free-for-all.*

> **Simultaneously:*

*WALLY: Don't push me!

*DENNY: Get in line. Get in line!

*EUGENE: Don't step on my marching foot!

LOIS cuts them off.

LOIS: Hey!

THEY stop arguing and snap to attention <u>one by one</u> as SHE calls them out.

Larry! Curly! Moe! We only have two days to get you into shape. Why don't you show me what you've been working on?

DENNY: You got it. *(Grudgingly magnanimous)* Duke, why don't you sing lead for now? I'll help the guys in the back row.

DUKE: Sure thing.

DENNY sets up the chair DR, motioning for WALLY to escort LOIS to the chair. DUKE crosses to EUGENE.

Eugene - remember what I told you to imagine?

EUGENE: Underwear. Underwear.

DUKE: Don't do it now.

EUGENE looks at LOIS, gets embarrassed and looks away.

DUKE grabs the tennis racket to use as a mic.

#7: LONELY TEARDROPS

DUKE:	**DENNY, EUGENE & WALLY:**
HEY	SHOO, BE, DO, WAH, WAH, WAH
HEY	SHOO, BE, DO, WAH, WAH, WAH
HEY	SHOO, BE, DO, WAH, WAH, WAH
MY HEART IS CRYIN', CRYIN'	

EUGENE tries hard to avoid looking at LOIS throughout the entire song. This goofs him up, causing the others to goof up.

DENNY and WALLY try to impress LOIS at every turn.

LONELY TEARDROPS	SHOO, WAH, WAH, WAH
MY PILLOW NEVER DRIES OFF	SHOO, WAH, WAH, WAH
LONELY TEARDROPS	SHOO, WAH, WAH, WAH
COME HOME	SHOO, WAH, WAH, WAH
COME HOME	AH—
JUST SAY YOU WILL	

DENNY and WALLY now bump into EUGENE numerous times with EUGENE yelping successively louder.

SAY YOU WILL	SAY YOU WILL
SAY YOU WILL	SAY YOU WILL
HEY, HEY	SAY YOU WILL

> *DENNY, EUGENE and WALLY crash into each other, causing a riot.*

> *DUKE crosses to LOIS.*

DUKE (CONT'D): See? It's hopeless.

> *LOIS jumps in to help.*

LOIS: Listen boys, right now you're all over the place.

> *THEY cross to LOIS to get instruction.*

Try to keep it simple. Keep it low.

> *SHE illustrates.*

Keep it cool.

DENNY: Like the Jets in West Side Story!

> *THEY all perform a 'Jets' move from "West Side Story:" DENNY coming forward to take the lead; WALLY is stiff; EUGENE hides behind the bar.*

LOIS *(to Denny)*: Just remember to do it all together, like a group.

> *DENNY pulls back to the group. SHE crosses to WALLY.*

(To Wally)

Try to twist your hips more, Wally. Like a hula hoop.

> *WALLY begins swiveling his hips, like he's working a massive hula hoop.*

Keep going!

> *SHE crosses to EUGENE who is hiding behind the bar.*

(To Eugene)

Eugene, what are you doing under there?

EUGENE *(popping up)*: Under wear?

> *HE realizes what HE said.*

Aahhh!

> *EUGENE shields his eyes and runs to the other side of the stage.*

LOIS *(following)*: Just keep it cool, Eugene, keep it cool.

> *EUGENE turns, sees her in her 'underwear,' and instantly becomes 'cool' as he snaps while staring/leering at her.*

> *DUKE frantically signals to EUGENE not to think of underwear.*

> *LOIS crosses back to DUKE.*

LOIS (CON'TD) *(to Duke)*: Let's see if that helps.

DUKE:	**DENNY, EUGENE & WALLY:**
JUST GIVE ME	
ANOTHER CHANCE	AH—
FOR OUR ROMANCE	AH—
COME ON AND TELL ME	AH—
THAT ONE DAY YOU'LL RETURN	YOU'LL RETURN—
BECAUSE EVERYDAY THAT	AH—
YOU'VE BEEN GONE AWAY	AH—

> *DUKE tosses away his tennis racket.*

> *DUKE rips open his work shirt, revealing his t-shirt underneath.*

YOU KNOW MY HEART DOES
NOTHIN' BUT BURN, CRYIN'

> *DUKE tosses his shirt toward the chair near LOIS.*

> *During the following verse, LOIS moves among the BOYS, helping them keep it low and cool.*

LONELY TEARDROPS	SHOO, WAH, WAH, WAH
MY PILLOW NEVER DRIES OFF	SHOO, WAH, WAH, WAH
LONELY TEARDROPS	SHOO, WAH, WAH, WAH
COME HOME	SHOO, WAH, WAH, WAH
COME HOME	AAH—

LOIS: Follow me, boys!

> *LOIS dances, DENNY, EUGENE and WALLY follow along, doing pretty well with her leading them.*

DUKE:	**DENNY, EUGENE & WALLY:**
JUST SAY YOU WILL	
SAY YOU WILL	SAY YOU WILL
HEY, HEY	SAY YOU WILL
SAY IT RIGHT NOW, BABY	SAY YOU WILL
SAY YOU WILL	SAY YOU WILL

> *DUKE now joins in the dance, and they begin to look like an honest-to-goodness do-wop singing group for the first time.*

SAY YOU WILL	SAY YOU WILL
SAY YOU WILL	SAY YOU WILL
JUST SAY YOU WILL	SAY YOU WILL

> *THEY all take a final pose.*

> *DUKE crosses to where he tossed his shirt.*

DENNY, EUGENE and WALLY gather around LOIS, speaking in quick succession.

DENNY: That was amazing!

EUGENE: I didn't realize how good we could be.

WALLY: You're just like Arthur Murray, but in a dress.

DENNY *(to Wally and Eugene)*: Let's go practice!

DENNY, WALLY & EUGENE cross to practice by the bar.

LOIS turns to DUKE.

DUKE: See what I mean?

LOIS: You're right. They'll never be dancers. We should just have them sing in the back, and you dance up front. You're in great shape.

DUKE bends over to get his shirt. SHE looks at his rear end as he bends over.

Really great shape.

DUKE: Thanks.

HE picks up his shirt.

LOIS: Is that song about anyone special?

DUKE: No one special, Miss Franklin. Just a song.

DUKE crosses away to the bar.

WALLY crosses in.

WALLY: So, do you think we'll be ready?

LOIS: I do. *(To all of them)* I think you're all doing...

THEY all lean in, hopeful. SHE offers them the best compliment she can.

... relatively well.

THEY celebrate.

WALLY moves a little too close to LOIS.

WALLY: Relatively well! That's pretty good for a Preacher's kid, right?

LOIS: Absolutely. If you just learn to twist those hips a bit more we'll have you dancing like Elvis in no time.

WALLY grabs LOIS' hand.

WALLY: Thank you, Lois.

HE swivels his hula hoop hips, doing his best/worst Elvis impersonation.

Thank you very much.

HE holds her hand close and tight.

WALLY (CONT'D): Soft...

LOIS *(trying to pull her hand back)*: Wally...!

WALLY *(looking at her)*: Super-duper soft...!

> *DENNY smacks WALLY in the shoulder, and WALLY lets go.*

> *LOIS crosses away, wiping her hand on her dress.*

DENNY: Smooth move... *(Imitating Wally's swivel hips)* ...lover boy.

WALLY *(upset at Denny)*: Lover boy. *(Dejected, kicking floor)* Lover boy. *(Thoughtful, with a smile)* Lover boy.

> *The bell tone in the music is WALLY's "lightbulb" moment: he looks out, and the world shifts around him.*

> *The lights shift dramatically on the bell tone to emphasize WALLY's dream world. The entire medley should feel like it's in the clouds, and the lights and effects achieve a floating/ethereal effect, placing this medley clearly in a fantasy world in their minds.*

#8: LOVIN' LOIS MEDLEY

[DEVIL OR ANGEL]

> *LOIS looks past each boy, never looking at them while they sing, always the perfect specimen of their dreams.*

> *Each soloist becomes the sort of perfect person they envision in their dreams, the one who would 'get the girl.'*

WALLY:	DENNY, DUKE & EUGENE:
	AHH—
DEVIL OR ANGEL	DEVIL OR ANGEL
I CAN'T MAKE UP MY MIND	AH—
WHICH ONE YOU ARE	WHICH ONE YOU ARE
I'D LIKE TO WAKE UP AND FIND	AH—
DEVIL OR ANGEL	DEVIL OR ANGEL
DEAR, WHICHEVER YOU ARE	AH—
I WANT YOU, I WANT YOU	WANT YOU, WANT YOU
I WANT YOU	WANT YOU
YOU LOOK LIKE AN ANGEL	OOH—
YOUR SMILE IS DIVINE	
BUT YOU KEEP ME GUESSING:	OOH—
WILL YOU EVER BE MINE	
DEVIL OR ANGEL	DEVIL OR ANGEL
PLEASE SAY YOU'LL BE MINE	AH—

WALLY (CONT'D):
LOVE ME OR LEAVE ME
I'M GOING OUT OF MY MIND
DEVIL OR ANGEL
DEAR, WHICHEVER YOU ARE
I LOVE YOU, I LOVE YOU
I-I LO-O-OVE YOU

DENNY, DUKE & EUGENE (CONT'D):
LOVE ME OR LEAVE ME
AH—
DEVIL OR ANGEL
AH—
LOVE YOU, LOVE YOU
I LOVE YOU

Dreamy music break.

LOIS crosses the stage.

AHH—

I LOVE YOU, MY DEVIL

The lights shift to DENNY's dream world, another hue of color.

[EARTH ANGEL]

DENNY:
OR ANGEL, EARTH ANGEL
COULD YOU BE MINE?
MY DARLING DEAR
I'D LOVE YOU ALL THE TIME
I'M JUST A FOOL
A FOOL IN LOVE WITH YOU

OH, I FELL FOR YOU
AND I KNEW
THE VISION OF YOUR LOVE'S
LOVELINESS
I HOPE AND I PRAY
THAT SOMEDAY
I'LL BE THE VISION
OF YOUR HAPPINESS

OH—
EARTH ANGEL, EARTH ANGEL
THE ONE I ADORE
LOVE YOU FOREVER
AND EVER AND EVER MORE
I'M JUST A FOOL
A FOOL IN LOVE WITH YOU
WOH

DUKE, EUGENE & WALLY:

OOH—
OOH—
OOH—
OOH, JUST A FOOL IN LOVE
IN LOVE WITH YOU

OH, OOH, FOR YOU
OOH, DOO WOP DOO WAH
OH
VISION OF LOVELINESS
OH
THAT SOMEDAY
VISION (VISION) (VISION)
OF YOUR HAPPINESS

OH—
EARTH ANGEL, EARTH ANGEL
(WOH) THE ONE I ADORE
I'LL LOVE YOU, WOH
FOREVER MORE
OOH, JUST A FOOL
IN LOVE, WOH—

DENNY (CONT'D):
A FOOL IN LOVE WITH YOU

> *The lights shift to EUGENE's dream world, yet another hue.*

[ONLY YOU]

EUGENE:	**DENNY, DUKE & WALLY:**
ONLY YOU CAN MAKE THIS	OOH
WORLD SEEM RIGHT	OOH
ONLY YOU CAN MAKE THE	OOH
DARKNESS BRIGHT	OOH, OOH
ONLY YOU AND YOU ALONE	AH
CAN THRILL ME LIKE YOU DO	AH
AND FILL MY HEART WITH LOVE	AH
FOR ONLY YOU	AH, FOR ONLY YOU
OH, OH
ONLY YOU CAN MAKE THIS	OOH
CHANGE IN ME	OOH

> *Upon singing the word "change," EUGENE whips off his glasses, turning from Clark Kent into a suave sort of Superman.*

FOR IT'S TRUE	OOH
YOU ARE MY DESTINY	OOH
WHEN YOU HOLD MY HAND	AH
I UNDERSTAND
THE MAGIC THAT YOU DO	AH, THAT YOU DO

> *EUEGENE puts his glasses back on.*

YOU'RE MY DREAM COME TRUE	AH
MY ONE AND ONLY YOU

> *The lights shift, to LOIS' dream world, another hue of color.*

[I ONLY HAVE EYES FOR YOU]

> *At first, we might believe LOIS is singing toward EUGENE.*

LOIS:
OUR LOVE MUST BE
A KIND OF BLIND LOVE
I CAN'T SEE ANYONE
BUT YOU

DENNY, DUKE, EUGENE & WALLY:
SHOO-BOP, SHOO-BOP
DOO-BOP SHOO-BOP

> *LOIS crosses toward DUKE, and the object of her fantasy becomes clear.*

LOIS:	**MEN:**
ARE THE STARS	SHOO-BOP, SHOO-BOP
OUT TONIGHT?	DOO-BOP SHOO-BOP
I DON'T KNOW IF IT'S	SHOO-BOP, SHOO-BOP
CLOUDY OR BRIGHT	DOO-BOP SHOO-BOP
I ONLY HAVE EYES	I ONLY HAVE EYES
FOR YOU, DEAR	FOR YOU, DEAR
THE MOON	SHOO-BOP, SHOO-BOP
MAY BE HIGH	DOO-BOP SHOO-BOP
BUT I CAN'T SEE A THING	SHOO-BOP, SHOO-BOP
IN THE SKY	DOO-BOP SHOO-BOP
'CAUSE I ONLY HAVE EYES	I ONLY HAVE EYES
FOR YOU	FOR YOU
I DON'T KNOW IF WE'RE IN A GARDEN	AH, AH
OR ON A CROWDED AVENUE	AH, AH
YOU ARE HERE	SHOO-BOP, SHOO-BOP
SO AM I	DOO-BOP SHOO-BOP
MAYBE MILLIONS OF	SHOO-BOP, SHOO-BOP
PEOPLE GO BY	DOO-BOP SHOO-BOP
BUT THEY ALL DISAPPEAR	BUT THEY ALL DISAPPEAR
FROM VIEW	FROM VIEW
AND I ONLY HAVE EYES	
FOR YOU	

> *WALLY, DENNY & EUGENE cross to LOIS.*

WALLY:	**DENNY, DUKE & EUGENE:**
DEVIL OR ANGEL	DEVIL OR ANGEL
PLEASE SAY YOU'LL BE MINE	AH—
DENNY:	**DUKE, EUGENE & WALLY:**
MY DARLING DEAR	OOH—
LOVE YOU ALL THE TIME	WHOA—
EUGENE:	**DENNY, DUKE & WALLY:**
YOU'RE MY DREAM COME TRUE	AH
MY ONE AND ONLY YOU—	

DENNY:
   I LOVE YOU
WALLY:
   I LOVE YOU
DENNY, EUGENE, WALLY & LOIS:
   I LOVE YOU

> *Button for applause.*
>
> *At top of applause, LOIS crosses to DUKE, puts her scarf around his neck, and kisses him.*
>
> *DENNY, EUGENE and WALLY stare, mouths agape.*
>
> *DUKE breaks away and moves toward getting his shirt to leave.*
>
> *After DUKE moves away, the BOYS jump in, speaking simultaneously*:*

*WALLY: My turn! My turn!

*DENNY: Don't forget me!

*EUGENE: Please, oh please, oh please...

> *DUKE grabs his shirt.*

LOIS: Duke... I'm sorry...!

> *LOIS moves toward DUKE, the BOYS move aside, so all can watch DUKE's exit.*

DUKE: Miss Franklin— I told you I need my job!

> *DUKE rushes up the stairs and exits (taking her scarf with him). The door slams shut behind him.*
>
> *There is a short pause.*

LOIS: Denny, do you have a powder room where I can freshen up?

DENNY: Of course, it's right through here. Back around to the left.

> *WALLY & EUGENE follow her as SHE exits.*

   Hey guys! Back off!

> *EUGENE & WALLY quickly move to separate places in the room.*
>
> *MRS. VARNEY opens the door and enters.*

LIGHTS: Lights flashing.

MRS. VARNEY (LIVE FROM OFFSTAGE): Dennis!

DENNY: What is it, Ma?

MRS. VARNEY (LIVE FROM OFFSTAGE): That young man just about bowled me over on his rush out of here.

DENNY: Sorry Ma.

MRS. VARNEY (LIVE FROM OFFSTAGE): And that young lady's rich parents are here to pick her up.

DENNY: She'll be up in a minute.

MRS. VARNEY (LIVE FROM OFFSTAGE): No lip, young man— don't keep them waiting. They're driving a Cadillac and probably don't feel comfortable in this part of town.

DENNY: Okay, okay!

MRS. VARNEY (LIVE FROM OFFSTAGE): And I found out about your fake job at the soda fountain, Denny. You've certainly got some explaining to do. If you think you can just sing and dance your life away while...(the rest of us make an honest living...)

       DENNY slams the door, cutting her off mid-sentence.

DENNY: Nag, naggedy-naggerson.

       LOIS enters from the powder room.

LOIS: Are my parents here?

       The BOYS all rush forward, speaking at once*.

*WALLY: No! I don't think so.

*DENNY: Of course not.

*EUGENE: I haven't seen anybody.

LOIS: Boys, I really have to go. My father— your sponsor— does not like to be kept waiting.

       SHE starts up stairs.

       DENNY grabs her and turns her back into the room.

#9: STAY

DENNY:	**EUGENE & WALLY:**
STAY JUST A LITTLE BIT LONGER	STAY, STAY

LOIS: Denny, there's just no way, Daddy's very impatient.

DENNY:	**EUGENE & WALLY:**
PLEASE, PLEASE, PLEASE,	PLEASE
PLEASE, PLEASE	
TELL ME YOU'RE GOING TO	

LOIS: Boys, I really have to go now. They're waiting.

WALLY:	**DENNY & EUGENE:**
NOW YOUR DADDY WON'T MIND	WAH, WAH, WAH
	DON'T TELL YOUR
	DADDY NOW
AND YOUR MOMMA WON'T MIND	WAH, WAH, WAH

WALLY (CONT'D):

IF WE HAVE ANOTHER DANCE, YEAH

JUST A-ONE MORE

EUGENE:

OH WON'T YOU STAY

JUST A LITTLE BIT

LONGER

PLEASE LET ME

HEAR

YOU SAY THAT YOU WILL

SAY YOU WILL

DENNY & EUGENE (CONT'D):
DON'T TELL YOUR
MOMMA NOW
WAH, WAH, WAH, WAH, WAH
A-ONE MORE, ONE MORE TIME

DENNY & WALLY:
BOP, BOP, BOP, WAH-OOH
BOP, BA DA DA DA
BOP, BOP, BOP, WAH-OOH
BOP, BA DA DA DA
BOP, BOP, BOP, WAH-OOH
BOP, BA DA DA DA
SAY YOU WILL

LOIS: You boys are going to get me into trouble. I still live at home, so I have rules I have to follow.

SOUND: Car honking from outside.

SHE grabs her sweater.

That's it. Daddy waits for no one. We'll pick up practice in the same place tomorrow night.

> *LOIS heads up the steps. On the landing/stairs, she turns and blows a kiss to each of the boys one by one and then exits.*
>
> *THEY each catch their kiss one by one, with WALLY catching the last one and holding it toward his lips for his first line.*
>
> *DENNY, EUGENE and WALLY continue singing as if LOIS were there in front of them, back in their imaginary dream world.*

WALLY:

WON'T YOU PRESS YOUR SWEET LIPS TO MINE

DENNY:

WON'T YOU SAY YOU LOVE ME

EUGENE:

ALL OF THE TIME

WHOA, YEAH, JUST A LITTLE BIT

LONGER

PLEASE, PLEASE, PLEASE, PLEASE

TELL-A ME YOU'RE GOIN' TO

DENNY & WALLY:
HUH, HUH!
STAY
WON'T YOU STAY A LITTLE BIT?
STAY
COME ON, JUST A LITTLE BIT?
PLEASE
PLEASE JUST A LITTLE BIT?
PLEASE
PLEASE JUST A LITTLE BIT?

DENNY:

    YOUR DADDY WON'T MIND

    YOUR MOMMA WON'T MIND

    IF YOU STAY AROUND
    AND HELP US, YEAH
    YOU COULD STAY ALL
    ALL NIGHT LONG!
    OH, STAY!

EUGENE & WALLY:

    WAH-OOH
    IF HE DON'T FIND OUT
    WAH-OOH
    IF SHE DON'T FIND OUT

    YEAH
    YOU COULD STAY ALL
    ALL NIGHT LONG!
    OH, STAY!

Blackout.

#9A: STAY PLAYOFF

ACT I, SCENE 4

FRIDAY EARLY EVENING.

> *SOUND: In the dark we hear the radio over the music playoff from the previous scene:*

DISC JOCKEY (V.O.): Hey cool cats! This is "Bullseye" Miller!

> *SOUND: "Arrow hitting a bullseye" sound effect.*

There's just one more day 'til we razz your berries and flap your jacks at the big Whopper Radio Rock 'n' Roll Roundup!

> *SOUND: Radio Jingle: "Big Whopper Radio."*

Get your tickets now at Pretty Peggy's Pet Paradise, where Pretty Peggy says, "If your new pet isn't purebred, your next puppy is freeeeeee!" And for one ginchy group of groovy guys and gals out there— winning the "Dream of a Lifetime" Talent Search will be the biggest thing since Elvis put on his blue suede shoes! You could be America's next big recording stars! Don't delay— sign up today!

> *LIGHTS up.*

> *DENNY, EUGENE and WALLY wear matching bowling shirts, with a bowling emblem on the front and DENNY and the DREAMERS emblazoned on the back.*

#10: JUST LIKE ROMEO & JULIET

DENNY:

	EUGENE & WALLY:
	OOH-OOH-OOH

FINDIN' A JOB TOMORROW MORNIN'
GOT A LITTLE SOMETHIN' I WANNA DO
GONNA BUY SOMETHIN' I COULD RIDE IN
TAKE MY GIRL DATIN' AT THE DRIVE-IN
OUR LOVE'S GONNA BE
WRITTEN DOWN IN HISTORY
JUST LIKE ROMEO AND JULIET

> *EUGENE and WALLY begin a clapping rhythm.*

	OOH-OOH-OOH
	DOO, DOOT, DOOT
	DOO, DOO, DOOT, DOO
I'M GONNA BUY HER PRETTY PRESENTS	OOH—
JUST LIKE THE ONES IN A CATALOG	OOH—

DENNY (CONT'D):

    GONNA SHOW HER HOW MUCH I LOVE

    LET HER KNOW ONE WAY OR THE OTHER

    OUR LOVE'S GONNA BE

    WRITTEN DOWN IN HISTORY

    JUST LIKE ROMEO AND JULIET

EUGENE & WALLY (CONT'D):

GONNA SHOW

LET HER KNOW

OH

OH—

JUST LIKE ROMEO AND JULIET

THEY add the clapping rhythm over the following.

DENNY:

    DOO, DOOT, DOOT,

    DOO, DOO, DOO, DOOT, DOO

    JUST LIKE ROMEO AND JULIET

    JUST LIKE ROMEO AND JULIET

    JUST LIKE ROMEO AND JULIET

    JUST LIKE ROMEO AND JULIET

    TALK ABOUT LOVE AND ROMANCE

    JUST WAIT 'TIL I GET MYSELF STRAIGHT

    I'M GONNA PUT ROMEO'S FAME

    RIGHT SMACK-DAB OUTTA A DATE

    AH, ALL RIGHT, NOW, I'M SPECULATIN'

    WONDER WHAT TOMORROW'S

    GONNA REALLY BRING

    IF I DON'T FIND WORK TOMORROW

    IT'S GONNA BE

    HEARTACHES 'N' SORROW

    OUR LOVE'S GONNA BE

    DESTROYED LIKE A TRAGEDY

    JUST LIKE ROMEO AND JULIET

    DOO, DOOT, DOOT, DOO

    DOO, DOO, DOOT, DOO

    JUST LIKE ROMEO AND JULIET

    JUST LIKE ROMEO AND JULIET

    JUST LIKE ROMEO AND JULIET

    JUST LIKE ROMEO AND JULIET

EUGENE & WALLY:

OOH-OOH-OOH

DOO, DOOT, DOOT

DOO, DOO, DOO, DOOT, DOO

JUST LIKE ROMEO AND JULIET

JUST LIKE ROMEO AND JULIET

JUST LIKE ROMEO AND JULIET

JUST LIKE ROMEO AND JULIET

IF I DON'T

GONNA BE

OH

OH—

JUST LIKE ROMEO AND JULIET

OOH-OOH-OOP

DOO, DOOT, DOOT, DOO

DOO, DOO, DOOT, DOO

JUST LIKE ROMEO AND JULIET

JUST LIKE ROMEO AND JULIET

JUST LIKE ROMEO AND JULIET

JUST LIKE ROMEO AND JULIET

DENNY (CONT'D):	EUGENE & WALLY (CONT'D):
OUR LOVE'S GONNA BE	
WRITTEN DOWN IN HISTORY	HISTORY, HISTORY
HISTORY, HISTORY	HISTORY, HISTORY
JUST LIKE ROMEO AND JULIET!	JUST LIKE ROMEO AND JULIET!

> *Button for applause.*

> *LIGHTS shift.*

> *DENNY admires himself in the mirror above the bar.*

WALLY *(to Denny)*: Okay, here's the deal. If Lois turns you down for a date, I'm next in line.

EUGENE: That's not fair! I've known her for the longest.

WALLY: But I have a car, and you only have a bus pass. Besides, you already had your turn at the school carnival. That counts, so you have to wait another cycle until it comes back to you.

EUGENE: Cycle? What do you mean "wait another cycle?" *(Turning to Denny for help)* Denny, he's not being fair!

DENNY: Why don't you drop a dime and tell someone who cares?

> *EUGENE protests with a noise.*

Why would Lois go out with either of you loser-doozers? Do you really think she'll turn down Denny from Denny and the Dreamers? *(Posing admiringly)* Look at me, will ya?

EUGENE: You look just like us.

WALLY: We're wearing the same thing.

DENNY: But I look cool in it.

EUGENE: Well, you're still living in your Mom's basement, and that's not cool.

WALLY: Yeah— you're not exactly a prime candidate for the dating market.

> *DUKE rushes in and down the stairs, closing the door behind him. HE is in his work clothes, wearing his leather jacket, which says "DUKE" on the back.*

> *HE is distressed about something, even though the BOYS don't seem to notice.*

EUGENE: Hi Duke.

WALLY: Hi Duke.

DUKE: Hi fellas.

DENNY: Hey— how'd you get past my Mom?

DUKE: Is Miss Franklin here?

DENNY: You're both late. So we started without you.

EUGENE: Boy, your heels were on fire last night!

WALLY: No doubt. We thought maybe you got "girl cooties" or something.

EUGENE and WALLY laugh.

DENNY pulls DUKE in close for some brotherly advise.

DENNY: I used to get nervous in front of girls too. But I'm pretty good at it now. So if you ever need any advice, I'm your "go-to guy."

DUKE: I'll keep that in mind.

DUKE steps back, looking at the BOYS.

Hey— are you guys going bowling?

DENNY: No. It's for the contest. Look.

THEY all turn in unison, showing off the backs of the shirts.

DENNY turns back to DUKE.

Hey, listen, maybe you can help us with something.

DUKE: I'll try.

DENNY: Since you clearly took yourself out of the running with Lois last night, she's now free to choose between the three of us.

DUKE: What on earth are you talking about?

DENNY: From a purely objective standpoint, who do you think stands the best chance?

DENNY, EUGENE and WALLY pose for DUKE.

DUKE: That's not how it works, Denny.

DENNY: Whattaya mean? You're out, I'm in. Works for me.

DUKE: Miss Franklin is from a very nice family. Her folks are particular about who she goes out with.

EUGENE: Lois and I already have a history. I think her parents will respect that.

DENNY: She can't even remember your name, dipstick!

WALLY: But I have a car. Her folks will like that, right?

DUKE puts his jacket down on the counter.

DUKE: Listen, fellas, you're barking up the wrong tree. Things don't always work out the way you want them to. Real love is tough. You can't just 'kick the tires' and take it out for a quick spin.

DENNY: I never know what the hell you're talking about.

DUKE: You think you're the right guy for Lois?

DENNY: Sure. Why not?

DUKE: What about her parents?

DENNY: Who cares about her parents?

DUKE: That's where you're not thinking straight, Denny. If her folks don't approve, the whole thing falls apart.

DENNY: Then we'll keep it quiet. Nobody needs to know.

DUKE: That's a dead end too. What's the point of hiding the most important part of your life? When you find the right girl, you'll want to shout it from the rooftop.

WALLY: So, how do you find the right girl?

DUKE: That, my friend, is the sixty-four thousand dollar question.

#11: A SUNDAY KIND OF LOVE

> *(Cont'd; singing)*
> I WANT A SUNDAY KIND OF LOVE
> A LOVE TO LAST PAST SATURDAY NIGHT
> I NEED TO KNOW IT'S MORE THAN LOVE AT FIRST SIGHT
> I WANT A SUNDAY KIND OF LOVE
>
> I WANT A LOVE THAT'S ON THE SQUARE
> CAN'T SEEM TO FIND SOMEBODY TO CARE
> I'M ON A LONELY ROAD THAT LEADS TO NOWHERE
> I WANT A SUNDAY KIND OF LOVE

Music continues under scene.

WALLY: You're talking about the perfect girl.

DENNY: Does she really exist?

EUGENE: Sure. My mom.

DENNY: You really are a loser-doozer, you know that?

WALLY: Well, I think she's out there. She just has to be.

DUKE: You think so?

WALLY: Oh sure. I think there's a perfect someone for every boy. There has to be. Otherwise, what chance do I have?

DUKE:	**WALLY:**
MY ARMS NEED SOMEONE TO ENFOLD	SOMEONE TO ENFOLD
TO KEEP ME WARM	AAH—
WHEN MONDAYS ARE COLD	

DUKE & WALLY:
A LOVE FOR ALL MY LIFE TO HAVE AND TO HOLD
I WANT A SUNDAY KIND OF LOVE

Button for applause.

DUKE: Shoot.

WALLY: Double shoot.

EUGENE & WALLY *(quickly to each other)*: Triple shoot!

THEY finger shoot at each other, all the way to the death.

DUKE: Listen fellas, I have something I need to tell you.

DENNY: What? More riddles about girls?

MRS. VARNEY opens the door and enters.

LIGHTS: *Lights flashing.*

MRS. VARNEY (LIVE FROM OFFSTAGE): Denny! That saucy young girl is here again!

WALLY and DENNY scramble to attention.

EUGENE runs to the stairs.

EUGENE: Thank golly! Send her down! Send her down!

EUGENE reaches up and slams the door.

HE realizes he was 'rude,' then shouts after.

Goodbye!

DENNY *(to Wally & Eugene)*: Now remember— I get first shot. Don't goof everything up.

WALLY: I've got second dibs.

EUGENE: History! We have history!

DUKE grabs his jacket.

DUKE: I should leave.

LOIS opens the door and enters, leaving the door open behind her.

The BOYS scramble to greet her.

LOIS: Boys, have you seen...

DUKE steps in.

DUKE: Miss Franklin.

LOIS: Duke! I rushed over as soon as I heard.

DENNY: Why? What did we miss?

DUKE and LOIS are oblivious to the others.

LOIS: My father can be very pigheaded.

DUKE: I warned you this would happen.

DENNY: What happened?

DUKE turns to DENNY, EUGENE & WALLY.

DUKE: Fellas, I have to leave the group.

DENNY: Whattaya mean, leave the group?

DUKE: Something came up.

DENNY: In the last ten seconds?

WALLY: The contest is tomorrow night!

EUGENE: We need you! Desperately!

DUKE: Sorry, fellas. *(To Lois)* I know my place, and I just don't fit in.

LOIS: Duke, please...!

DUKE turns back to DENNY, EUGENE & WALLY.

DUKE: That's it, Denny. I'm out of the group.

DENNY: Throwing in the towel. Just what I expected from a grease-monkey hood from the wrong side of town.

DUKE: Denny, that's not fair...

DENNY: See if I care! We'll do the contest without you!

EUGENE: But we can't, Denny, we can't.

WALLY: Yeah. He sings best in the low parts. My mouth hurts when I sing way down there.

DUKE starts for the stairs.

LOIS: If you walk out now, it just proves everything Daddy says is true!

DUKE turns back to her.

DUKE *(upset)*: Your father is...

HE stops himself.

(Resigned)

Your father is right.

DUKE rushes up the stairs.

SHE runs to the bottom of the stairs and calls after him.

LOIS: And don't ever come back!

DUKE pauses, then shuts the door and exits.

LOIS crosses away from the stairs, facing out, softly crying.

WALLY *(whispering to Denny & Eugene)*: Second dibs. *(Still whispering, yet more emphatically)* Second dibs!

DENNY: It's just as well he's gone, Lois. We can do way better than a hooligan on a Harley.

LOIS: Not now, Denny.

DENNY notices LOIS is crying.

DENNY: I'm sorry. As my mother would happily point out to you, I'm slightly insensitive to the emotional needs of women.

LOIS turns and really sees the BOYS for the first time.

LOIS: Are you guys going bowling?

DENNY: No. I got them for the contest. Look!

THEY all turn in unison, showing off the back of the shirts.

LOIS: Sorry, Denny. Daddy wants you to wear outfits promoting the auto shop.

DENNY: Well maybe Daddy doesn't always get what he wants.

LOIS: That is exactly what I said to him last night. And then all hell broke loose.

EUGENE & WALLY *(low and quiet, interested)*: Oooooh...!

LOIS: You see, I never told Daddy about Duke being in the group.

EUGENE: You didn't?

LOIS: And Daddy pulled up last night just in time to see Duke leaving.

WALLY: That's not good.

LOIS: So we had quite a scene in the car. Daddy was screaming, calling Duke all sorts of terrible things— and the whole time Mom is crying hysterically.

DENNY: I've made Mom cry— that's never good.

LOIS: We drove home in complete silence. I went straight to my room, but I couldn't sleep. I was up all night, tossing and turning— I just couldn't quite figure it out.

DENNY: Figure what out?

LOIS: I was so angry at Daddy, but it was something else. Something I didn't even understand myself, because it happened so quickly. But when I got up this morning it washed over me like a tsunami.

SHE is excited and thrilled to finally tell everyone.

I got dressed, went downstairs and told Mom and Daddy that I was absolutely sure.

The boys are listening intently.

(Proudly, resolutely)

I am in love with Duke.

DENNY: Shoot.

WALLY: Double shoot.

EUGENE & WALLY *(quietly to each other)*: Triple shoot...

EUGENE and WALLY feebly finger shoot at each other once.

#12: UNCHAINED MELODY

LOIS: When I said it out loud, Daddy got up and walked straight out of the house. When Duke went to work today, Daddy fired him. No explanation— he just told him to clean out his locker and get out. So, Duke lost his job, you lost your lead singer, and I lost my chance. I made a mess of everything.

LOIS (CONT'D):

    LONELY RIVERS FLOW
    TO THE SEA, TO THE SEA
    TO THE OPEN ARMS OF THE SEA

        LOIS now sings out, to DUKE.

    OH, MY LOVE, MY DARLING
    I HUNGER FOR YOUR TOUCH
    A LONG, LONELY TIME
    TIME GOES BY SO SLOWLY
    AND TIME CAN DO SO MUCH
    WILL YOU BE MINE?
    I NEED YOUR LOVE
    I NEED YOUR LOVE
    GOD SPEED YOUR LOVE TO ME

        The song has a false ending, and the lights fade.

        The intro vamp for DUKE's section segues on the applause.

        The lights rise on DUKE on the opposite side of the stage. He is wearing his leather jacket, talking on a payphone.

DUKE: Hey, Russ. It's Duke Henderson, Molly's boy.

        He listens.

Yeah, I miss her too. You know, I promised Mom that I was gonna make something of my life—that I'd always make her proud. Something happened today that, well... I'm in kind of a bad situation. Have you got any work down at the dock? Short term, long term—whatever you've got.

        He listens.

Sure, I've still got my bike. I'll be there first thing in the morning. I'll tell you all about it.

        HE hangs up. LIGHTS down on DUKE.

        LIGHTS up on LOIS on the opposite side of the stage from DUKE.

LOIS:

    LONELY RIVERS CRY
    "WAIT FOR ME, WAIT FOR ME
    I'LL BE COMING HOME, WAIT FOR ME!"

        LIGHTS up on DUKE.

DUKE:	**DENNY, EUGENE & WALLY:**
OH, MY LOVE, MY DARLING	OH, MY LOVE, MY DARLING
I'VE HUNGERED FOR YOUR TOUCH	OOH
A LONG, LONELY TIME	OOH, SUCH A LONELY TIME

DUKE (CONT'D):
AND TIME GOES BY SO SLOWLY
AND TIME CAN DO SO MUCH
COULD YOU BE MINE?

DENNY, EUGENE & WALLY (CONT'D):
OH
OOH
ARE YOU MINE?

The song drives to the end.

LOIS:
I NEED YOUR LOVE

DUKE:
I NEED YOUR LOVE

LOIS & DUKE:
GOD SPEED YOUR LOVE TO ME

DENNY, EUGENE & WALLY:
AAH—

Blackout.

END OF ACT I

INTERMISSION

ACT II

#13: ENTR'ACTE

SCENE 1

LATE SATURDAY MORNING.

#14: DREAMIN'

The music begins in the dark.

DENNY, EUGENE & WALLY:
OOH—
OOH—

Special on DENNY.

DENNY:
DREAMIN'
I'M ALWAYS DREAMIN'
DREAMIN'
LOVE WILL BE MINE

Special on EUGENE.

EUGENE:	**DENNY:**
SEARCHIN'	OOH—
I'M ALWAYS SEARCHIN'	OOH—
HOPIN'	OOH—
SOMEDAY I'LL FIND	OOH—

Special on WALLY.

WALLY:	**DENNY & EUGENE:**
SOMEONE	AAH—
SOMEONE TO LOVE ME	AAH—
SOMEONE TO NEED ME	AAH—
BUT UNTIL THEN	AAH—

Lights up to reveal them rehearsing in the basement, LOIS watching.

DENNY:	**EUGENE & WALLY:**
I'LL KEEP ON	
DREAMIN'	DREAMIN', OOH—
KEEP RIGHT ON DREAMIN'	DREAMIN', OOH—
DREAMIN'	DREAMIN', OOH, WAH

DENNY (CONT'D):   **EUGENE & WALLY (CONT'D):**
   TILL MY DREAMIN' COMES TRUE— OOH—
   OOH—   OOH—
     (Giving directions; speaking)
  2, 3, 4!
     (Singing)
   OOH—   OOH—

     Music continues.

     DENNY crosses to LOIS.

DENNY: So? Whattaya think? We still got it, right?

LOIS: I think we need to withdraw from the contest.

DENNY: No! We worked all night on this song.

LOIS: It's just that...

DENNY: Wait. We can do it better!

     DENNY turns around and visually gives the guys a demanding pep talk. THEY now sing with exaggerated gestures and movements. DENNY speaks dramatically as the guys doo-wop behind.

DENNY *(speaking):*   **EUGENE & WALLY** *(singing):*
   DREAMIN'   DOOT-DOOT, DOOT
                                  SHOOP-DOO-WAH
   I'M ALWAYS DREAMIN'   DOOT-DOOT, DOOT
                                  SHOOP-DOO-WAH
   DREAMIN'   DOOT-DOOT, DOOT
                                  SHOOP-DOO-WAH
   LOVE WILL BE MINE   MI-YI-YI-YI-YI

     DENNY gestures to EUGENE and WALLY to 'give it their all.'

     THEY double-down on their gestures.

   SEARCHIN'   DOOBY-DOO-WAH, SHOOP-DO-WAH
   I'M ALWAYS SEARCHIN'   DOOBY-DOO-WAH, SHOOP-DO-WAH
   HOPIN'   DOOBY-DOO-WAH, SHOOP-DO-WAH
   SOMEDAY I'LL FIND   FI-YI-YI-YI-YI
     (Singing)
   SOMEONE   YAAH—
   SOMEONE TO LOVE ME   YAAH—
   SOMEONE TO NEED ME   YAAH—
   BUT UNTIL THEN—   BUT UNTIL THEN—

DENNY (CONT'D):	DENNY & EUGENE:
WELL I'LL KEEP ON DREAMIN'	JUST DREAMIN' SHOOP-DO-WAH
KEEP RIGHT ON DREAMIN'	JUST DREAMIN' SHOOP-DO-WAH
DREAMIN'	WE'RE DREAMIN' DO-WAH
TILL MY DREAMIN' COMES TRUE—	OOH—

(Speaking)

C'mon, fellas!

(Singing)

OOH—	OOH—

(Speaking)

Bigger!

(Singing)

OOH—	OOH—
DREAMIN' OF YOU!	DREAMIN' OF YOU!
ZOOT-DO-WAH	ZOOT-DO-WAH

Button for applause.

The BOYS all gather round LOIS, waiting for her reaction.

DENNY: So?

LOIS: Interesting.

DENNY *(to Eugene and Wally)*: Made in the shade!

WALLY: I knew it!

EUGENE: Told ya so.

LOIS: I said it was interesting, Denny, but it's still missing something.

WALLY: I knew it!

EUGENE: Told ya so.

LOIS: It's just missing a certain je ne sais quoi, you know?

DENNY: How would I know what Joony-Shoo-whatchamacallit means?

EUGENE: I think it's French for Duke.

LOIS: Well it's just not working without him. Besides, you're registered as a quartet for the contest.

DENNY: Okay, fine. If you say we need Duke, then you have to bring him back.

LOIS: Duke is gone. He cut out on the group, remember? He said he didn't fit in.

DENNY: I don't think he would've left if he knew how you felt. Go find him and tell him that he's the one.

LOIS: Enough, Denny. It's not that simple. Daddy's right. Duke and I just don't go together.

EUGENE: Of course you go together.

WALLY: You go together like ham and eggs.

EUGENE: Like macaroni and cheese.

WALLY: Like biscuits and gravy. *(Exploding)* Man, I'm hungry!

> *WALLY leads EUGENE toward the stairs, ad-libbing about getting sandwiches from the kitchen before being stopped by DENNY.*

DENNY: Can it, fellas! *(To Lois)* Listen, Lois. The contest is tonight and we need Duke. There's no more time to think about it. Sometimes you just have to make some noise and take a stand!

#15: EASIER SAID THAN DONE

Simultaneously.

*DENNY: You've gotta tell him how you feel!

*EUGENE: We really need him in the group!

*WALLY: Go find him and bring him back!

LOIS:	DENNY, EUGENE & WALLY:
MY FRIENDS ALL TELL ME	
GO TO HIM, RUN TO HIM	GO, GO
SAY SWEET LOVELY THINGS TO HIM	RUN, RUN
AND TELL HIM - HE'S THE ONE	TELL HIM— HE'S THE ONE
DEEP IN MY HEART I KNOW IT	OOH—
BUT IT'S SO HARD TO SHOW IT	OOH—
'CAUSE IT'S EASIER	EASIER
EASIER SAID THAN DONE	SAID THAN DONE
MY BUDDIES TELL ME	
FLY TO HIM, SIGH TO HIM	FLY, FLY
TELL HIM I WOULD DIE FOR HIM	SIGH, SIGH
TELL HIM - HE'S THE ONE	TELL HIM— HE'S THE ONE
ALTHOUGH HE GIVES ME A FEELING	OOH—
THAT SETS MY HEART A-REELING	OOH—
YET IT'S EASIER	EASIER
EASIER SAID THAN DONE	SAID THAN DONE

LOIS (CONT'D):

WELL, I KNOW THAT I LOVE HIM SO

I'M AFRAID THAT HE'LL NEVER KNOW

BECAUSE I, I FEEL SO NERVOUS INSIDE

TO FIND HIM AND

LOOK HIM IN THE EYE

THEY ALL TELL ME

SING TO HIM, SWING WITH HIM

AND JUST DO ANYTHING FOR HIM

TELL HIM - HE'S THE ONE

I WANT A LOVE SO TRUE

AND I'M SAD AND BLUE

'CAUSE IT'S EASIER

EASIER SAID THAN DONE

WELL, YOU KNOW THAT I LOVE HIM SO

I'M AFRAID THAT HE'LL NEVER KNOW

BECAUSE I, I

FEEL EMBARRASSED AND SHY

I JUST CAN'T LOOK HIM IN THE EYE

THEY ALL TELL ME

GO TO HIM, RUN TO HIM

GET HIM BACK TO SING WITH THEM

TELL HIM - HE'S THE ONE

I FOUND A LOVE SO TRUE

YET I'M SAD AND BLUE

'CAUSE IT'S EASIER

EASIER SAID THAN DONE

DENNY, EUGENE & WALLY (CONT'D):

I KNOW, UH-HUH

OOH—

I, I

FIND HIM AND

LOOK HIM IN THE EYE

SING, SING

SWING, SWING

TELL HIM— HE'S THE ONE

OOH—

OOH—

EASIER

SAID THAN DONE

WE KNOW, UH-HUH

OOH—

I, I

LOOK HIM IN THE EYE

GO, GO

RUN, RUN

TELL HIM— HE'S THE ONE

OOH—

OOH—

EASIER

SAID THAN DONE

The BOYS all speak simultaneously*:

*DENNY: You've gotta just find him and tell him to come back!

*EUGENE: Duke is the answer to all of our problems!

*WALLY: We need him in the group, no ifs, ands or buts.

LOIS W/ DENNY, EUGENE & WALLY:

EASIER-ER-ER-ER SAID THAN DONE

Button for Applause.

DENNY, EUGENE and WALLY surround LOIS.

EUGENE: We really do need Duke. He was the glue that held us all together. *(Backtracking with Lois)* Besides you, that is. He's just regular glue. You're super glue.

WALLY: There's no such thing as super glue, dummy.

EUGENE: Well, there oughta be.

> *A light bulb goes off for EUGENE. HE thinks earnestly about it for a moment, then dismisses it.*

No.

> *WALLY heads to the bar, where a plate of Twinkies awaits.*

LOIS: I'm sorry about the contest, boys. I know you were looking forward to it.

DENNY: Mom'll just have to wait a few more years to get her sewing room back, I guess.

> *DENNY turns away, dejected.*

LOIS: You'll get your chance, Denny. You can do anything when you put your mind to it. You're a natural-born leader. These boys— they'd follow you anywhere. That's quite a gift.

DENNY *(touched, even embarrassed by her praise)*: Thanks, Lois.

> *LOIS turns to Eugene.*

LOIS: Eugene — you should take the Cadillac out of the garage a little more often! I've never seen anyone improve so quickly.

EUGENE: Duke gave me a secret weapon, and I've been using it all night. It really seems to be working.

LOIS: Well whatever it is...

> *SHE turns toward the others, and EUGENE looks at her backside.*

...keep doing it.

> *When SHE turns back, EUGENE gives her a big 'thumbs up' with a grin.*
>
> *LOIS turns to WALLY at the bar, who is already holding a Twinkie.*

And Wally — you've become quite the dancer. Very light on your feet.

WALLY *(holding out a Twinkie)*: I've been watching what I eat.

> *WALLY takes a generous bite (possibly the entire Twinkie in one bite).*
>
> *EUGENE moves forward with a prepared speech, but it all seems to go wrong.*

EUGENE: Lois, I know you don't like us the way we like you. Well, not anymore. I mean, we don't like you like that anymore. I mean, I do, well, I did, in fifth grade, but, not like that, and, well, I still do, but, uh, you, uhm...

HE stammers about. SHE touches him lightly, which calms him.

LOIS: Eugene. If I was mean to you back in school, it's only because I didn't know any better. But I know better now. You are one of the finest gentlemen I've ever met. *(To all of them)* You're all terrific young men. I'm so happy we've become such good friends.

DENNY: We're happy too. Before you came along, we were just three dopey guys singing in my Mom's sorry old basement. You taught us that we could dream our dreams and shouldn't be laughed at because of it. You taught us to be better friends. You taught us to work together.

DENNY takes her hand.

You're our magic ingredient.

#16: (YOU'VE GOT) THE MAGIC TOUCH

DENNY: **EUGENE & WALLY:**
YOU-OO-VE GOT THE MAGIC TOUCH
IT MAKES ME GLOW SO MUCH
IT CASTS A SPELL, IT RINGS A BELL

HE rings the bell by the bar on the beat.

THE MAGIC TOUCH   OOH—

OH-UH-OH WHEN I FEEL YOUR CHARM   OOH—
IT'S LIKE A FOUR-ALARM   OOH—
YOU MAKE ME THRILL SO MUCH   OOH—
YOU'VE GOT THE MAGIC TOUCH   OOH—

WALLY: **DENNY & EUGENE:**
IF I GO REELING, UH-OH,   OH—
I'M FEELING THE GLOW   UH-OH
BUT WHERE CAN I GO FROM YOU   OOH—

DENNY: **EUGENE & WALLY:**
I DIDN'T KNOW TOO MUCH   OOH—
AND THEN I FELT YOUR TOUCH   OOH—
AND NOW I'VE LEARNED I CAN RETURN   OOH—
THE MAGIC TOUCH   OOH—

EUGENE: **DENNY & WALLY:**
IF I GO REELING, UH-OH,   OH—
I'M FEELING THE GLOW   UH-OH
BUT WHERE CAN I GO FROM YOU   OOH—

DENNY: **EUGENE & WALLY:**
WE DIDN'T KNOW TOO MUCH   OOH—
AND THEN WE FELT YOUR TOUCH   OOH—

DENNY (CONT'D):
AND NOW WE'VE LEARNED
WE CAN RETURN
THE MAGIC TOUCH

EUGENE & WALLY (CONT'D):
OOH—
OOH—

EUGENE, DENNY & WALLY:
THE MAGIC TOUCH
WE LOVE YOU
WE LOVE YOU
WE LOVE YOU

Button for applause.

THEY surround HER.

LOIS: Okay, okay! We can't just sit here. One way or another, you boys have got to perform at that contest!

DENNY: Will you come sing with us? You can be our fourth!

*EUGENE and WALLY eagerly agree, pleading
simultaneously.

*EUGENE: Oh, my golly, yes! You know all the moves!

*WALLY: That'd be really super-duper-swell-and-a-half!

LOIS: Oh, no, no, no! That'd really make Daddy blow a gasket!

DENNY: Who cares what your father says? Make some noise. Stand out in the crowd. I've been defying my mother for years and I turned out okay.

LOIS laughs.

LOIS: You know, Denny, you're right! You boys go get dressed for the contest—your new outfits from Big Stuff are upstairs.

*WALLY and EUGENE run up the stairs, followed by DENNY,
who waits near the bottom of the stairs.*

Then wait for me here. And keep practicing!

DENNY: Where are you going?

LOIS: I'm going to go make some noise and take a stand.

The boys celebrate and exit, closing the door behind them.

#17: LONELY TEARDROPS (REPRISE)

LOIS crosses SR, and the lights focus tight on her.

(Cont'd; singing)
JUST GIVE ME A SECOND CHANCE
FOR OUR ROMANCE
COME ON AND TELL ME
THAT ONE DAY YOU'LL RETURN

LOIS (CONT'D):
BECAUSE EVERY DAY THAT
YOU'VE BEEN GONE AWAY
YOU KNOW MY HEART DOES
NOTHING BUT BURN

> *DUKE appears SL, in front of his wall. HE is holding LOIS'*
> *scarf.*

> *THEY both sing out.*

DUKE:
YOU KNOW MY HEART DOES
NOTHING BUT BURN

LOIS:	**DUKE:**
CRY-YI-YI-YI-ING	CRY-YI-YI-YI-ING
LONELY TEARDROPS	LONELY TEARDROPS
MY PILLOW NEVER DRIES OFF	
'CAUSE I'M CRYIN'	
LONELY TEARDROPS	LONELY TEARDROPS
COME HOME	'CAUSE I ONLY HAVE EYES
	FOR YOU—
JUST SAY YOU WILL	
SAY YOU WILL	OUR LOVE HAS
	GOTTA BE BLIND
SAY YOU WILL	I SEE NOBODY BUT YOU
OH, THE MOON IS OUT TONIGHT	SAY YOU WILL
THE STARS ARE SHINING BRIGHT	OH, SAY YOU WILL
SAY YOU WILL	

LOIS & DUKE:
JUST SAY YOU WILL

> *Blackout.*

#17: LONELY TEARDROPS PLAYOFF

ACT II, SCENE 2

SATURDAY AFTERNOON: AN HOUR LATER.

> *SOUND: In the dark we hear the radio, over the playoff from the previous scene:*

DISC JOCKEY (V.O.): Hey cool cats — This is "Bullseye" Miller!

> *SOUND: "Arrow hitting a bullseye" sound effect.*

This is it! Tonight's the night we're cooking with gas at the big Whopper Radio Rock 'n' Roll Round-up!

> *SOUND: Radio Jingle: "Big Whopper Radio."*

So, buy your tix, take your licks, hop in the mix, and get your kicks!

> *The playoff ends, followed by the new music:*

#18: BUZZ BUZZ BUZZ

You'll see every group sing onstage tonight in this year's big talent search, brought to you by yours truly and Bullseye Records!

> *SOUND: "Arrow hitting a bullseye" sound effect.*

So bring some green and make the scene, 'cuz Life Could Be A Dreamy Dream!!

> *LIGHTS up on DENNY, EUGENE & WALLY, rehearsing together.*
>
> *THEY are wearing matching auto-shop-style coveralls, with the "Big Stuff Auto" logo on the back, and embroidered name badges on the front.*

DENNY, EUGENE & WALLY:
WAH-OOH, WAH-OOH
WAH-OOH, WAH-OOH

DENNY:
WELL BUZZ, BUZZ, BUZZ GOES THE BUMBLE BEE
TWIDDLEE-DEEDLEE-DEE GOES THE BIRD
BUT THE SOUND OF YOUR LITTLE VOICE, DARLING
IS THE SWEETEST SOUND I'VE EVER HEARD
I'VE SEEN THE BEAUTY OF THE RED, RED ROSE
SEEN THE BEAUTY WHEN THE SKY IS BLUE
I'VE SEEN THE BEAUTY OF THE EVENING SUNSET

DENNY (CONT'D):
BUT THE BEAUTY OF YOU!
SWEET IS THE HONEY FROM THE HONEYCOMB
SWEET ARE THE GRAPES FROM THE VINE
BUT THERE'S NOTHING AS SWEET AS YOU, DARLING
AND I HOPE SOME DAY YOU'LL BE MINE!

Music continues underneath.

DENNY: Now this is where we show off the outfits.

THEY turn together, showing the back of the coveralls.

DENNY, EUGENE & WALLY:
BIG STUFF

THEY face front again.

DENNY: And now for the people on that side.

THEY turn and show their backs again.

DENNY, EUGENE & WALLY:
BIG STUFF

THEY face front again. EUGENE continues dance moves with military precision.

WALLY: I dunno, Denny. Duke had that extra something when he sang the song.

DENNY: Well he's not here. Do you see him? I don't see him.

WALLY: But if Duke's not in front, I vote we split up the solo part.

DENNY: This is not a democracy. It's called Denny and the Dreamers. *(Pointing to his name badge)* Denny.

WALLY: But I've been working really hard on my twist and I want everyone to see.

EUGENE: C'mon, Denny. Give him a chance.

DENNY: Fine.

DENNY crosses to the bar to get the bee hat.

You can be 'the bee.'

DENNY places a hat shaped like a bee on WALLY's head.

WALLY, DENNY & EUGENE:
BUZZ, BUZZ
WAH-OOH, WAH-OOH
WAH-OOH, WAH-OOH

WALLY:
WELL BUZZ, BUZZ, BUZZ GOES THE BUMBLE BEE
TWIDDLEE-DEEDLEE-DEE GOES THE BIRD

WALLY (CONT'D):
>BUT THE SOUND OF YOUR LITTLE VOICE, DARLING
>
>IS THE SWEETEST SOUND I'VE EVER HEARD

DENNY: Make it bounce!

>*WALLY bounces extravagantly, making the antenna, the wings, and the legs all bounce.*

WALLY:
>I'VE SEEN THE BEAUTY OF THE RED, RED ROSE
>
>SEEN THE BEAUTY WHEN THE SKY IS BLUE
>
>I'VE SEEN THE BEAUTY OF THE EVENING SUNSET
>
>BUT THE BEAUTY OF

EUGENE & WALLY:
>OOH!
>
>SWEET IS THE HONEY FROM THE HONEYCOMB
>
>SWEET ARE THE GRAPES FROM THE VINE

WALLY:
>BUT THERE'S NOTHING AS SWEET AS YOU, DARLING
>
>AND I HOPE SOME DAY YOU'LL BE MINE!

EUGENE & WALLY:
>HOPE SOME DAY YOU'LL BE MINE!

DENNY, EUGENE & WALLY:
>HOPE SOME DAY YOU'LL BE MINE!

>*THEY face back for their final pose, bumping their bums and showing the back of the coveralls for the final "Buzz Buzz."*

>BUZZ, BUZZ

>*Button for applause.*

>*WALLY points to the antenna.*

WALLY: I don't wanna wear this stupid thing.

EUGENE: That Spelling Bee hat means a lot in this town.

WALLY: It's stupidy-stupid.

EUGENE: You're stupidy-stupid!

DENNY: If you wanna have the bee solo, you gotta be 'the bee.'

WALLY: I don't wanna be 'the bee.' Everyone at the Piggly Wiggly is gonna laugh.

EUGENE: That's because you dance funny.

>*EUGENE grabs the hat from WALLY.*

WALLY: But Denny said, "make it bounce!"

EUGENE: Not like Tigger the Tiger!

> *EUGENE puts the hat on his head and illustrates,*
> *extravagantly.*

WALLY: I was just following the leader. *(To Denny)* You said bounce, so I did.

DENNY: But you bounced like you had a super-wedgie.

EUGENE: Ha!

DENNY: And Eugene, you goofed the double-step-hop move again.

WALLY: Ha!

EUGENE: What are you talking about? I did it perfectly. Every single time.

> *EUGENE illustrates, bee hat bouncing with each step.*

DENNY: I thought it was messy, that's all.

EUGENE: Lois loves the way I dance!

> *EUGENE takes off the bee hat, gestures with it.*

Just because you lost your "bee" solo doesn't mean you can take it out on me.

DENNY: Do the move right next time, and I won't have a problem.

> *EUGENE mumbles back angrily at DENNY. THEY grunt at*
> *each other, then retreat to different areas of the basement.*
>
> *There is a moment of silence.*

DENNY: I miss Lois.

EUGENE: Me too.

WALLY: I miss Duke.

EUGENE: Me too.

> *DENNY crosses center.*

DENNY: I may be stating the obvious here, but we don't need a Duke. We've got a Denny! And after we win that contest, Ed Sullivan's gonna fight with Dick Clark to see who gets me first!

> *DUKE enters, leaving the door open, racing down the stairs.*
> *HE is wearing his leather jacket over his A-shirt.*

DUKE: Hey fellas.

WALLY: The prodigal mechanic returns!

EUGENE: You showed up just in time!

WALLY: No doubt!

DENNY: We thought you were gone for good.

DUKE: So did I.

> *DUKE notices THEIR matching coveralls.*

Are you guys fixing a flat or something?

DENNY: No — they're for tonight. Look!

> *DENNY, EUGENE & WALLY turn in unison to show DUKE the back of their coveralls.*

DENNY, EUGENE & WALLY: Buzz buzz!

DUKE: Fellas, I need to apologize.

EUGENE *(confidently moving forward)*: No, we need to apologize to you. If Denny offended you in any way, he's incredibly sorry.

DENNY: Hey!

> *EUGENE holds up his hand to stop DENNY's protest.*

EUGENE: You should know, Duke, that we are completely open-minded about motorcycles, leather jackets, and hoodlums from the wrong side of town.

> *EUGENE knows he blew it, kicks the floor and moves aside.*
>
> *WALLY moves in to give it a try.*

WALLY: What he means is, we treat everyone equally. Even hooligans.

> *WALLY knows he's miffed it, and kicks the floor.*
>
> *WALLY and EUGENE cross away.*

DENNY: Ignore them. They don't have the best social skills. What the hell am I talking about? I don't have the best social skills.

> *DUKE and DENNY share a laugh.*

Eugene is right. I didn't mean anything I said last night. I was being the biggest loser-doozer of all.

DUKE: It's alright. You know, yesterday I was ready to ditch everything and get back to my old life... *(Playfully to Eugene & Wally)* ...as a hooligan on the wrong side of town... *(Back to Denny)* But then I got to thinking: I was just starting to like my new life. When I was growing up I always promised Mom that someday I was going to make her proud. I'm pretty sure that 'someday' starts tonight, singing with you guys.

EUGENE & WALLY *(sweetly, simply)*: Aaaaww.

DUKE: And here's what I really need to say. Mom always taught me to do what's right, no matter what. I didn't do that with you guys. I got scared, so I ran. And for that, I'm sorry. When Mom passed away last year, I came here to start over. I got the job at Big Stuff Auto and just tried to do the best I could. But no matter what I did, I never seemed to fit in.

> *EUGENE crosses close to DUKE, stares at him for a second, then wraps him in a bear hug.*
>
> *DUKE looks for help, unable to breathe.*
>
> *WALLY pries EUGENE free.*

WALLY: You fit in with us, Duke. If we made you feel bad, we didn't mean it. We were in the glee club at high school, so we know what it feels like to be outsiders.

EUGENE hugs DUKE again.

WALLY pulls him off again.

DUKE: So the only thing I have to do now is fix everything with Lois. I thought I had everything under control, but she sorta sideswiped me, ya know? I never saw it coming.

DUKE pulls out LOIS' scarf from his pocket.

#19: FOOLS (REPRISE)/THE GLORY OF LOVE

[FOOLS FALL IN LOVE (REPRISE)]

(Cont'd; singing)
FOOLS FALL IN LOVE IN A HURRY
WHEN THEY SHOULD BE PLAYING IT COOL
I USED TO LAUGH BUT NOW I UNDERSTAND
SHAKE THE HAND OF A BRAND NEW FOOL

Music continues under.

(Speaking)

I was a fool for running away. I should have stood up to Earl. I should have stood up for myself. I can't imagine I have a chance with Lois now.

WALLY: You've got way more than a chance, my friend. Forget about Earl. None of that truly matters if the two of you love each other. You've found someone pretty special— no doubt at all. You can't walk away from it. You just can't.

[THE GLORY OF LOVE]

(Cont'd; singing)
YOU'VE GOT TO GIVE A LITTLE
TAKE A LITTLE
AND LET YOUR POOR HEART
BREAK A LITTLE
THAT'S THE STORY OF
THAT'S THE GLORY OF LOVE

	DENNY & EUGENE:
YOU'VE GOT TO LAUGH A LITTLE	OOH
CRY A LITTLE	OOH—
AND LET THE CLOUDS ROLL BY A LITTLE	OOH

WALLY (CONT'D):	**DENNY & EUGENE (CONT'D):**
THAT'S THE STORY OF	OOH
THAT'S THE GLORY OF LOVE	OOH

LOIS enters on the stairs, unseen.

DUKE crosses DR, facing out.

DUKE:
AS LONG AS THERE'S THE TWO OF US
WE'VE GOT THE WORLD AND ALL ITS CHARMS
AND WHEN THE WORLD IS THROUGH WITH US
I'LL HOLD HER IN MY ARMS

DUKE puts the scarf in his pocket.

WALLY:	**DENNY & EUGENE:**
YOU'VE GOT TO WIN A LITTLE	OOH
LOSE A LITTLE	OOH—
AND ALWAYS HAVE THE BLUES A LITTLE	OOH
THAT'S THE STORY OF	OOH
THAT'S THE GLORY OF LOVE	OOH

DENNY, EUGENE, WALLY & DUKE:
THE GLORY OF LOVE

DENNY, EUGENE & WALLY surround DUKE.

Button for applause.

DUKE: Fellas, I have to quit running. It's time to shout it from the rooftop.

LOIS has moved downstage, unseen by the boys.

LOIS: You were saying...?

DENNY, EUGENE and WALLY jump and turn with a loud yelp, surprised.

DUKE: Lois!

LOIS: Yes?

DUKE *(nervous, to Wally)*: What was I saying?

WALLY: Speak from the heart.

DUKE steps toward LOIS and hesitates.

DUKE: I've never been so nervous in my life.

EUGENE *(loud whisper to Duke)*: Underwear!

DENNY & WALLY smack EUGENE on the arm.

#20: LIFE COULD BE A DREAM (REPRISE)/DUKE OF EARL

[LIFE COULD BE A DREAM (REPRISE)]

> *LOIS steps to DUKE and places her finger on his lips.*
>
> *SHE sings in tempo rubato, ad libitum.*

LOIS:
LIFE COULD BE A DREAM
IF YOU WOULD TAKE ME UP TO PARADISE ABOVE
IF YOU WOULD TELL ME I'M THE ONLY ONE THAT YOU LOVE
LIFE WILL BE A DREAM, SWEETHEART

> *The music segues.*

[DUKE OF EARL]

> *(Cont'd; speaking)*

You know, there's just enough time for you to change so we can get to that contest.

DUKE: It seems to me we've got all the time in the world.

> *WALLY crosses and sings toward LOIS, then toward DUKE.*

WALLY:
DUKE, DUKE, DUKE, DUKE OF EARL
DUKE, DUKE, DUKE OF EARL
DUKE, DUKE, DUKE OF EARL
DUKE, DUKE, DUKE OF

> *The others join in.*

DENNY, EUGENE & WALLY:
DUKE, DUKE, DUKE, DUKE OF EARL
DUKE, DUKE, DUKE OF EARL
DUKE, DUKE, DUKE OF EARL
DUKE, DUKE, DUKE OF EARL

DUKE:	**DENNY, EUGENE & WALLY:**
AS I	DUKE, DUKE, DUKE OF EARL
WALK THROUGH THIS WORLD	DUKE, DUKE, DUKE OF EARL
NOTHING CAN STOP	DUKE, DUKE, DUKE OF EARL
THE DUKE OF EARL	DUKE, DUKE, DUKE OF EARL
I WANT YOU	DUKE, DUKE, DUKE OF EARL
FOR MY GIRL	DUKE, DUKE, DUKE OF EARL
SO, NO ONE CAN HURT YOU	DUKE, DUKE, DUKE OF EARL
OH NO	DUKE, DUKE, DUKE OF

DUKE (CONT'D): DENNY, EUGENE & WALLY (CONT'D):

YES, I, YOU KNOW I'M GONNA AAH—

LOVE YOU, OH, OH, COME ON, LET ME AAH—

HOLD YOU DARLIN', AAH—

'CAUSE I'M THE DUKE OF

EARL AAH—

SO YEAH, YEAH, YEAH, YEAH BUM, BA-BA BUM, BA-BA

BA-BA-BA-BA BUM, BUM

DUKE gets out LOIS' scarf from his jacket pocket.

AND WHEN I DUKE, DUKE, DUKE OF EARL

HOLD YOU DUKE, DUKE, DUKE OF EARL

YOU'LL BE MY DUCHESS DUKE, DUKE, DUKE OF EARL

DUCHESS OF EARL DUKE, DUKE, DUKE OF EARL

WHEN I WALK DUKE, DUKE, DUKE OF EARL

THROUGH MY DUKEDOM DUKE, DUKE, DUKE OF EARL

I SEE THE PARADISE DUKE, DUKE, DUKE OF EARL

THAT WE WILL SHARE DUKE, DUKE, DUKE OF

DUKE returns LOIS' scarf to her before the end of the chorus.

I, YOU KNOW I'M GONNA AAH—

LOVE YOU, OH, OH AAH—

NOTHING CAN STOP ME, DARLING AAH—

'CAUSE I'M THE DUKE OF EARL AAH—

BUM, BA-BA BUM, BA-BA

BA-BA-BA-BA BUM, BUM

Music continues under.

(Speaking)

Lois, I can't offer you riches and wealth. But I can offer you something more: my heart. And no matter what...

DUKE gets down on one knee.

I'll always treat you like royalty.

LOIS toys with DUKE a bit, making him wait.

LOIS:

OH YES, AT LAST IN THIS WORLD

I'VE GOT THE DUKE, THE DUKE OF EARL

LOIS circles around DUKE, taking his leather jacket and putting it on.

AND I, I AM HIS GIRL

AND NO ONE CAN HURT ME, OH NO

LOIS helps DUKE up from his knee.

SHE ties her scarf around his neck.

LOIS: **DENNY, EUGENE & WALLY:**

LOIS	DENNY, EUGENE & WALLY
YES, I, I'M GOING TO LET YOU	AAH—
LOVE ME, OH, OH	AAH—
NO ONE CAN HURT ME NOW	AAH—

LOIS turns to show off Duke's name on the back of his jacket.

'CAUSE I'M THE DUCHESS OF EARL	AAH—
UH, YEAH, YEAH, YEAH, YEAH	BUM, BA-BA BUM, BA-BA
	BA-BA-BA-BA BUM, BUM
OOH, OOH, OOH, OOH	DUKE, DUKE, DUKE OF EARL
OOH, OOH—	DUKE, DUKE, DUKE OF EARL
	DUKE, DUKE, DUKE OF EARL
AAH, AAH, AAH—	DUKE, DUKE, DUKE OF

DUKE & LOIS: **DENNY, EUGENE & WALLY:**

DUKE & LOIS	DENNY, EUGENE & WALLY
OOH, OOH, OOH, OOH	DUKE, DUKE, DUKE OF EARL
OOH, OOH—	DUKE, DUKE, DUKE OF EARL
	DUKE, DUKE, DUKE OF EARL
AAH, AAH, AAH—	DUKE, DUKE, DUKE OF

ALL:

OOH, OOH, OOH, OOH

OOH, OOH—

AAH, AAH, AAH

DUKE OF EARL

DUKE swings LOIS into an embrace and THEY kiss on the final button.

Blackout.

ACT II, SCENE 3

THE FINALE

In the blackout a sparkly curtain with four walk-through splits covers the stage.

In the dark, we hear:

ANNOUNCER (V.O.): Ladies and gentlemen, this is "Bullseye" Miller.

> *SOUND: "Arrow hitting a bullseye" sound effect.*

After a triumphant American tour of the lower 48, and back in Springfield for one night only, I'm happy as a humpback whale to bring to the stage your very own home-grown recording stars and winners of the big "Dream of a Lifetime" Talent Search from Bullseye Records and Whopper Radio.

> *SOUND: Radio Jingle: "Big Whopper Radio."*

Oh, wait a minute, I have a special guest to help with this next part.

MRS. VARNEY (V.O.): Hello Springfield, this is Denny's mother, Mrs. Varney. Can you believe it? My boy is a big star! I always knew he could do it! I never doubted him, not for a second. I always said to him, I said, "Denny. Why get a job? You can sing for a living!" That's what I said. So, without any further ado, whatever the heck that means, let's bring out my boys!

#21: PRETTY LITTLE ANGEL EYES

Here they are: Denny & The Dreamers!

> *Rock 'n' roll curtain warmer lights come on, revealing the curtain.*

> *Spots ballyhoo on the curtain.*

DUKE:
PRETTY LITTLE ANGEL EYES
DUKE & WALLY:
PRETTY LITTLE ANGEL EYES
DUKE, WALLY & EUGENE:
PRETTY LITTLE ANGEL, PRETTY LITTLE ANGEL
DUKE, WALLY, EUGENE & DENNY:
PRETTY LITTLE, PRETTY LITTLE
PRETTY LITTLE ANGEL

> *Full lights up as DENNY, DUKE, EUGENE and WALLY enter sharply and simultaneously through the slits in the curtain, wearing matching jackets with red shirts. THEY are in full-on star mode.*

DUKE, WALLY & DENNY: **EUGENE:**
  EYES   OOH—
  DOO-WAH, OH, OH, OH, OH   OOH—
DUKE, WALLY & DENNY: **EUGENE:**
  OOH-WAH   OOH—
DUKE:
  PRETTY LITTLE, LITTLE, LITTLE ANGEL EYES
DENNY: **DUKE, EUGENE & WALLY:**
  ANGEL EYES   DOO-WOP, DOO-WOP
                                                      ANGEL EYES
  I REALLY LOVE YOU SO   OH, OH, OH, OH
  ANGEL EYES   DOO-WOP, DOO-WOP
                                                      ANGEL EYES
  I'LL NEVER LET YOU GO   OH, OH, OH, OH
  BECAUSE I LOVE YOU   DOO-WOP, DOO-WOP
  MY DARLING ANGEL EYES   DOO-WOP, DOO-WOP
                                                      OH ANGEL

DUKE:
  PRETTY LITTLE, LITTLE, LITTLE ANGEL EYES
DENNY: **DUKE, EUGENE & WALLY:**
  ANGEL EYES   DOO-WOP, DOO-WOP
                                                      ANGEL EYES
  YOU ARE SO GOOD TO ME   OH, OH, OH, OH
  AND WHEN I'M IN YOUR ARMS   DOO-WOP, DOO-WOP
                                                      ANGEL EYES
  YOU FEEL SO HEAVENLY   OH, OH, OH, OH
  YOU KNOW I LOVE YOU   DOO-WOP, DOO-WOP
  MY DARLING ANGEL EYES   DOO-WOP, DOO-WOP
                                                      OH ANGEL EYES

WALLY: **DENNY, DUKE & EUGENE:**
  I KNOW YOU WERE SENT   OOH—
  FROM HEAVEN ABOVE
  TO FILL MY LIFE   OOH—
  WITH YOUR WONDERFUL LOVE
EUGENE: **DENNY, DUKE & WALLY:**
  I KNOW WE'LL BE HAPPY FOR ETERNITY   OOH—
  'CAUSE I KNOW-OW-OW-OW-OW-OW-OW
  THAT OUR LOVE IS REALLY REAL—
DUKE:
  ANGEL EYES
DENNY: **EUGENE, DUKE & WALLY:**
  ANGEL EYES   DOO-WOP, DOO-WOP
                                                      ANGEL EYES

DENNY (CONT'D):	EUGENE, DUKE & WALLY (CONT'D):
I REALLY LOVE YOU SO	OH, OH, OH, OH
ANGEL EYES	DOO-WOP, DOO-WOP
	ANGEL EYES
I'LL NEVER LET YOU GO	OH, OH, OH, OH
BECAUSE I LOVE YOU	DOO-WOP, DOO-WOP
MY DARLING ANGEL EYES	DOO-WOP, DOO-WOP
	OH, ANGEL EYES

Music continues.

DENNY: Ladies and gentlemen, please welcome our own pretty little angel and newlywed, Mrs. Lois Henderson!

DENNY, EUGENE, DUKE & WALLY move to the side, gesturing as LOIS enters through a split in the center of the curtain, wearing a spectacular black dress with red trim and polka dots to match the MEN's outfits.

LOIS bows/curtseys.

DUKE places his mic center for LOIS as SHE steps forward to speak.

LOIS: Put your hands together for the amazing Big Dreamer Band!

The curtains rise to reveal the band. The back wall, stairs, and furniture have been removed. Hanging along the side are graphic sixties rock 'n' roll posters of "Denny & The Dreamers."

THEY all acknowledge the band.

DUKE joins LOIS, splitting the microphone center.

LOIS:	EUGENE, DENNY & WALLY:
ANGEL EYES	DOO-WOP, DOO-WOP
	ANGEL EYES
I REALLY LOVE YOU SO	OH, OH, OH, OH
DUKE:	**EUGENE, DENNY & WALLY:**
ANGEL EYES	DOO-WOP, DOO-WOP
	ANGEL EYES
I'LL NEVER LET YOU GO	OH, OH, OH, OH
LOIS:	**EUGENE, DENNY & WALLY:**
BECAUSE I LOVE YOU	DOO-WOP, DOO-WOP
	DOO-WOP, DOO-WOP
MY DARLING ANGEL EYES	OH ANGEL, PRETTY LITTLE
	LITTLE, LITTLE ANGEL EYES
DUKE:	**EUGENE, DENNY & WALLY:**
MY DARLING ANGEL EYES	OH ANGEL, PRETTY LITTLE
	LITTLE, LITTLE ANGEL EYES

LOIS & DUKE:	**EUGENE, DENNY & WALLY:**
MY DARLING ANGEL EYES	OH ANGEL EYES

Applause segue.

EUGENE moves forward, center mic.

DUKE brings on another mic, so each now have a mic on a stand.

#22: DO YOU LOVE ME?/THE TWIST

[DO YOU LOVE ME?]

EUGENE:
YOU BROKE MY HEART
'CAUSE I COULDN'T DANCE
YOU DIDN'T EVEN WANT ME AROUND
AND NOW I'M BACK TO LET YOU KNOW
I CAN REALLY SHAKE 'EM DOWN

LOIS joins the group; THEY all join in with backups.

	DUKE, DENNY, LOIS & WALLY:
DO YOU LOVE ME?	I CAN REALLY MOVE
DO YOU LOVE ME?	I'M IN THE GROOVE
NOW, DO YOU LOVE ME?	DO YOU LOVE ME?

ALL:
NOW THAT I CAN DANCE?

EUGENE:	**DUKE, DENNY, LOIS & WALLY:**
WATCH ME NOW, HEY	HEY, WORK, WORK
WORK IT OUT, BABY	WORK, WORK
WELL, YOU'RE DRIVING ME CRAZY	WORK, WORK
JUST A LITTLE BIT OF SOUL NOW	WORK
I CAN MASH POTATO	I CAN MASH POTATO
AND DO THE TWIST	I CAN DO THE TWIST
I CAN WAH, WATUSI	WAH, WATUSI
DO YOU LIKE IT LIKE THIS?	DO YOU LIKE IT LIKE THIS?
TELL ME, TELL ME	TELL ME
DO YOU LOVE ME?	DO YOU LOVE ME?
DO YOU LOVE ME?	DO YOU LOVE ME?
DO YOU LOVE ME?	DO YOU LOVE ME?

ALL:
NOW THAT I CAN DANCE?

The music segues immediately as WALLY comes forward, taking the center mic.

[THE TWIST]

WALLY:	DENNY, DUKE, EUGENE & LOIS:
COME ON BABY	OOH, WAH, WAH
LET'S DO THE TWIST	OOH, WAH, WAH
COME ON BABY	OOH, WAH, WAH
LET'S DO THE TWIST	OOH, WAH, WAH
TAKE ME BY MY LITTLE HAND	OOH, WAH
AND GO LIKE THIS	OOH, WAH, WAH
EH AH TWIST	ROUND & ROUND & ROUND & ROUND
BABY, BABY TWIST	ROUND & ROUND & ROUND & ROUND
OOH YEAH	ROUND & ROUND & ROUND & ROUND
JUST LIKE THIS	ROUND & ROUND & ROUND & ROUND
COME ON LITTLE MISS	OOH, WAH
AND DO THE TWIST	ROUND & ROUND & ROUND & ROUND
EH AH TWIST	ROUND & ROUND & ROUND & ROUND
BABY, BABY TWIST	ROUND & ROUND & ROUND & ROUND
OOH YEAH	ROUND & ROUND & ROUND & ROUND
JUST LIKE THIS	ROUND & ROUND & ROUND & ROUND
COME ON LITTLE MISS	OOH, WAH
AND DO THE TWIST	ROUND & ROUND & ROUND & ROUND

EUGENE:	DUKE, LOIS & WALLY:
DO YOU LOVE ME?	DO YOU LOVE ME?
DENNY:	**DUKE, EUGENE & LOIS:**
DO YOU LOVE ME?	DO YOU LOVE ME?
WALLY:	**DUKE, DENNY, EUGENE & LOIS:**
DO YOU LOVE ME?	DO YOU LOVE ME?

DENNY, EUGENE & WALLY:
NOW THAT I CAN DANCE?

ALL:
WORK! WORK!

Applause segue.

THEY rearrange once again, with DUKE moving forward.

#23: RAMA-LAMA DING DONG

DUKE:
RAMA LAM

DENNY, EUGENE, LOIS & WALLY:
DING DONG

DUKE:
RAMA LAM

DENNY, EUGENE, LOIS & WALLY:
DING, DING, DONG

DUKE:
RAMA LAMA, LAMA, LAMA, LAMA DING DONG
RAMA LAMA, LAMA, LAMA, LAMA DING

LOIS:	**DENNY, EUGENE, DUKE & WALLY:**
OOH—	RAMA LAMA, LAMA
	LAMA, LAMA DING DONG
OOH—	RAMA LAMA, LAMA
	LAMA, LAMA DING
OOH—	RAMA LAMA, LAMA
	LAMA, LAMA DING DONG
OOH—	RAMA LAMA, LAMA
	LAMA, LAMA DING
OOH—	RAMA LAMA, LAMA
	LAMA, LAMA DING DONG
OOH—	RAMA LAMA, LAMA
	LAMA, LAMA DING
OOH-WAH-OOH	OOH-WAH-OOH

DUKE:	**DENNY, EUGENE, LOIS & WALLY:**
OH, OH, OH, OH	
I GOT A	RAMA LAMA, LAMA
GIRL NAMED	LAMA, LAMA DING DONG
RAMA LAMA	RAMA LAMA, LAMA
RAMA LAMA DING DONG	LAMA, LAMA DING
SHE'S EV'RYTHING	RAMA LAMA, LAMA
TO ME	LAMA, LAMA DING DONG
RAMA LAMA	RAMA LAMA, LAMA

DUKE (CONT'D):   **DENNY, EUGENE, LOIS & WALLY (CONT'D):**

DUKE (CONT'D):	DENNY, EUGENE, LOIS & WALLY (CONT'D):
RAMA LAMA DING DONG	LAMA, LAMA DING
I'LL NEVER	RAMA LAMA, LAMA
SET HER FREE	LAMA, LAMA DING DONG
'CUZ SHE'S MINE	RAMA LAMA, LAMA
ALL MINE	LAMA, LAMA DING
	OOH-WAH-OOH
OH, OH, OH	[BOYS ONLY:] BOW BOW BOW
I GOT A	RAMA LAMA, LAMA
GIRL NAMED	LAMA, LAMA DING DONG
RAMA LAMA	RAMA LAMA, LAMA
RAMA LAMA DING DONG	LAMA, LAMA DING
SHE IS	RAMA LAMA, LAMA
FINE TO ME	LAMA, LAMA DING DONG
RAMA LAMA	RAMA LAMA, LAMA
RAMA LAMA DING DONG	LAMA, LAMA DING
YOU	RAMA LAMA, LAMA
WON'T BELIEVE	LAMA, LAMA DING DONG
THAT SHE'S MINE	RAMA LAMA, LAMA
ALL MINE	LAMA, LAMA DING
	OOH-WAH-OOH

DUKE:
    BOW BOW BOW BOW BOW BOW BOW

DENNY:	EUGENE, DUKE & WALLY:
WE LOVE HER, LOVE HER	OH— [BUM, BUM, ETC.]
LOVE HER SO	

WALLY:	DENNY, EUGENE & DUKE:
THAT WE'LL NEVER	OH— [BUM, BUM, ETC.]
NEVER LET HER GO	

EUGENE:	DENNY, DUKE & WALLY:
ONE THING IS CERTAIN	OH— [BUM, BUM, ETC.]
SHE USED TO BE MINE	

DUKE:	DENNY, EUGENE & WALLY:
NOW SHE'S MINE	SHE'S HIS
ALL OF THE TIME	OH, OH

DUKE:	DENNY, EUGENE, LOIS & WALLY:
I GOT A	RAMA LAMA, LAMA
GIRL NAMED	LAMA, LAMA DING DONG
RAMA LAMA	RAMA LAMA, LAMA
RAMA LAMA DING DONG	LAMA, LAMA DING

88 SH-BOOM! LIFE COULD BE A DREAM

DUKE (CONT'D):
SHE'S EV'RYTHING
TO ME
RAMA LAMA
RAMA LAMA DING DONG
I'LL NEVER
SET HER FREE
'CUZ SHE'S MINE
ALL MINE

DENNY, EUGENE, LOIS & WALLY (CONT'D):
RAMA LAMA, LAMA
LAMA, LAMA DING DONG
RAMA LAMA, LAMA
LAMA, LAMA DING
RAMA LAMA, LAMA
LAMA, LAMA DING DONG
RAMA LAMA, LAMA
LAMA, LAMA DING
OOH-WAH-OOH

Dance and music break.

BOW, BOW, BOW
RAMA LAM

DENNY, EUGENE, LOIS & WALLY:
DING DONG

DUKE:
RAMA LAM

DENNY, EUGENE, LOIS & WALLY:
DING, DING, DONG

DUKE:
BOW BOW BOW
I GOT A
GIRL NAMED
RAMA LAMA
RAMA LAMA DING DONG
I'LL NEVER
LET HER GO
RAMA LAMA
RAMA LAMA DING DONG
I LOVE HER
LOVE HER SO
AND SHE'S MINE
ALL MINE

BOW BOW BOW

LOIS:
OOH—

OOH—

DENNY, EUGENE, LOIS & WALLY:
[BOYS ONLY:] BOW BOW BOW
RAMA LAMA, LAMA
LAMA, LAMA DING DONG
RAMA LAMA, LAMA
LAMA, LAMA DING
RAMA LAMA, LAMA
LAMA, LAMA DING DONG
RAMA LAMA, LAMA
LAMA, LAMA DING
RAMA LAMA, LAMA
LAMA, LAMA DING DONG
RAMA LAMA, LAMA
LAMA, LAMA DING
OOH-WAH-OOH
[BOYS ONLY:] BOW BOW BOW

DENNY, DUKE, EUGENE & WALLY:
RAMA LAMA, LAMA
LAMA, LAMA DING DONG
RAMA LAMA, LAMA
LAMA, LAMA DING

LOIS (CONT'D):	DENNY, DUKE, EUGENE & WALLY (CONT'D):
OOH—	RAMA LAMA, LAMA
	LAMA, LAMA DING DONG
OOH—	RAMA LAMA, LAMA
	LAMA, LAMA DING
OOH—	RAMA LAMA, LAMA
	LAMA, LAMA DING DONG
OOH—	RAMA LAMA, LAMA
	LAMA, LAMA DING

DENNY, DUKE, EUGENE & WALLY:
OOH WAH
OOH WAH

LOIS:	DENNY, DUKE, EUGENE & WALLY:
OOH WAH	OOH WAH
YEAH!	RAMA LAMA,
	LAMA, LAMA, DING!

THEY all step to the side of their mics with one arm up and bow deeply on the final beat.

BLACKOUT.

Lights up.

This should be treated as an encore. Let the applause continue, as THEY ask if the audience wants "one more," etc.

#24: ENCORE: UNCHAINED MELODY (REPRISE)

DUKE:
BO, BO, BO, BO, BO, BO
BA-DUM, DUM, DUM, DUM

ALL:
OH MY LOVE, MY DARLING
I'VE HUNGERED FOR YOUR
T-T-T-T-T-TOUCH, OOOOOH
TIME GOES BY SO SLOWLY
AND TIME CAN DO SO
M-M-M-M-M-MUCH
ARE YOU STILL MINE—

LOIS:	DENNY, EUGENE, DUKE & WALLY:
I NEED YOUR LOVE	NEED IT, NEED IT, NEED IT
	NEED IT, NEED IT
I NEED YOUR LOVE	NEED IT, NEED IT, NEED IT
	NEED IT, NEED IT

LOIS (CONT'D):
   GODSPEED YOUR LOVE

DENNY, EUGENE, DUKE & WALLY (CONT'D):
   NEED IT, NEED IT, NEED IT

DUKE:
   YEAH, YEAH

DENNY, EUGENE, LOIS, WALLY:
   TO ME

DENNY, EUGENE, LOIS, WALLY:
   LONELY RIVERS FLOW TO THE SEA-EA

DUKE:
   YEAH, YEAH, FLOW, FLOW TO
   SEA, SEA LOOK AT THE SEA

TO THE OPEN ARMS

   C'MON PRETTY BABY
   DO YOU TO

OF THE SEA-EA

   OF THE SEA, SEA
   LOOK AT THE SEA

TIME

   C'MON PRETTY BABY
   ONE MORE TIME

NEAR THE SIDE

   NEAR THE SIDE, SIDE,
   WAIT FOR ME, ME
   WAIT FOR ME

WAIT FOR ME-EE

   I'LL BE COMIN' HOME
   MY BABY I'LL

I'LL BE COMIN' HOME, WAIT AND SEE—

   BE COMIN' HOME

ALL:
   OH MY LOVE, MY DARLING
   I HUNGER FOR YOUR
   T-T-T-T-T-T-TOUCH, OOOOH
   T-T-T-T-TOUCH, OOOOH
   T-T-T-T-TOUCH, OOOOH
   T-T-T-T-T-T-TOUCH, AAHH

      Blackout.

      Cast exits.

ANNOUNCER (V.O.): Ladies and gentlemen, let's hear it for Denny & the Dreamers!

      LIGHTS up.

#25: BOWS

      Cast enters one at a time for final bows:

      WALLY— EUGENE— DENNY— then LOIS and DUKE enter together.

      DUKE gives LOIS the final bow.

      THEY acknowledge the band.